LILLIAN TO
JENNIFEF

CW00894146

2011

fortune & feng shui

RaBBiT

Congratulations!

I want to thank and congratulate you for investing in yourself...and in the latest edition of Fortune and Feng Shui...your personalized horoscope book for 2011!

What will you be earning one year from today? How will you look and feel one year from today...and will you be happier?

In this little book Jennifer and I reveal many insights pertaining to your particular animal sign...what you can expect and how to protect and enhance all areas of your life for success in 2011.

And why stop here?

I'd like to also extend a personal invitation to you to join my Mandala...and receive my FREE online weekly newsletter...Lillian Too's Mandala Ezine.

You'll discover other powerful feng shui secrets from me that go hand-in-hand with the valuable information in this book. And it's absolutely FREE... delivered to your inbox weekly!

You've taken the first step to success by purchasing this book. Now expand your horizons and learn more about authentic feng shui that really works...including more about the powerful 3rd dimension...your inner feng shui!
Just go to www.lilliantoomandalaezine.com and register today!

Don't miss out! It's easy to register at www.lilliantoomanadalaezine.com and you'll also receive a special BONUS from me when you register today! I look forward to visiting with you online!

All the best!
Lillian

Fortune & Feng Shui 2011 RABBIT
by Lillian Too and Jennifer Too
© 2011 Konsep Lagenda Sdn Bhd

Text © 2011 Lillian Too and Jennifer Too
Photographs and illustrations © WOFS.com Sdn Bhd

The moral right of the authors to be identified as authors of this book
has been asserted.

Published by KONSEP LAGENDA SDN BHD (223 855)
Kuala Lumpur 59100 Malaysia

For more Konsep books, go to www.lillian-too.com or www.wofs.com
To report errors, please send a note to errors@konsepbooks.com
For general feedback, email feedback@konsepbooks.com

ISBN 978-967-329-040-6
Published in Malaysia, August 2010

RABBIT BORN CHART

BIRTH YEAR	WESTERN CALENDAR DATES	AGE	KUA NUMBER MALES	KUA NUMBER FEMALES
Earth Rabbit	19 Feb 1939 to 7 Feb 1940	72	7 West Group	8 West Group
Metal Rabbit	6 Feb 1951 to 26 Jan 1952	60	4 East Group	2 West Group
Water Rabbit	25 Jan 1963 to 12 Feb 1964	48	1 East Group	5 West Group
Wood Rabbit	11 Feb 1975 to 30 Jan 1976	36	7 West Group	8 West Group
Fire Rabbit	29 Jan 1987 to 16 Feb 1988	24	4 East Group	2 West Group
Earth Rabbit	16 Feb 1999 to 4 Feb 2000	12	1 East Group	5 West Group

CONTENTS

4. INTERACTING WITH OTHERS IN 2011

Relationship With Others Improve Despite Hostile Star

5. MONTHLY ANALYSES OF YOUR LUCK

Good Timing Help You Actualise Big Auspicous Luck

6. IMPORTANT FENG SHUI UPDATES FOR 2011

7. POWERFUL TALISMANS & AMULETS FOR 2011

RABBIT YEAR 2011
Clashing Elements
But Economically Better

The Year of the **Golden Rabbit** 2011 will be a noisy year filled with the sounds of clashing elements. Global energy continues to be discordant. But it is a year when most animal signs enjoy the potential to make genuinely good advances economically. There is money to be made. In fact, for those who are able to tap into their veins of good fortune, 2011 can turn out to be a bonanza year.

2011 is a year that favors animal signs located in the secondary compass directions and is less favorable to those occupying cardinal directions. So two thirds of the animal signs can look forward to improving their financial situation.

We examine three important indicators to determine the year's outlook when the diplomatic, soft-hearted Rabbit rules, taking center stage and bringing a new set of energies to the fortunes of the world. After the dramatic earthquakes, landslides and volcanic eruptions of the Tiger Year, can we welcome in a quieter, safer and more stable year? Alas, if the charts are any indication, it seems not; there are deep rumblings under the earth; natural disasters and discordant chi continues to pose a threat to our safety; these calamities threaten different parts of the world. Earth's environment needs time to settle but for most individuals, happily the outlook does not look that dire. There is more good luck than bad for most of the animal signs.

Outlook for the 12 Animals

In 2011, the cardinal East and West animal rulers, **Rabbit** and **Rooster**, are afflicted by harmful energy and need to stay alert. These two must watch their backs, as both signs are affected. East and West are strongly afflicted directions.

The **Rabbit** in 2011 is hit by the nasty *wu wang* or five yellow, which is a powerful and nasty feng shui affliction. This is a negative star number that brings ill winds of misfortune and it must be strongly subdued. Those born in the year of the Rabbit must protect themselves against this star affliction, which is so strong it is also reflected in the constellation of the 24 mountains. This is the annual affliction most feared by those who practice feng shui, and to have the animal sign that rules the year be afflicted by it is indeed not a good sign. The remedy for the *wu wang* that is needed therefore must be strong enough to overcome its power. Thus for 2011, we are bringing out a remedy - the **five element pagoda** - that also has the **tree of life** which symbolizes the supremacy of the Wood element of the Rabbit over the Earth element of the five yellow. This is the most important thing for the Rabbit to put in place - the cure for the *wu wang*!

The **Rooster** meanwhile sits on the *Disaster Energy* Star in the West and must contend with the *Three Killings* affliction. These are bad winds which must also be strongly subdued before Rooster can benefit from favorable feng shui brought by the number 9 star.

The **Snake** continues to have a good year in 2011 as it benefits from excellent feng shui winds. This is a year when continuous good fortune comes and brings big as well as small successes. The Snake enjoys excellent indications of good fortune brought by the 24 mountain stars. Snake will definitely be on a big roller coaster ride in 2011.

The Ox enjoys a wonderful year as it benefits from the double *Big Auspicious* stars that flank its astrological location. This together with its number 1 star ensures that good fortune manifests strongly. Meanwhile, inviting a deity figure into the home brings good luck, as the Ox has the *Golden Deity* Star in its chart this year.

The **Rat** and **Horse** also enjoy the promise of good fortune, but whether or not they can actually cause this good luck potential to materialize will depend on their own inventiveness. But doing well in 2011 does not come without a share of the year's discordance. The Horse has a tendency to get sick, while the Rat's normally calm demeanor is put out of sorts by quarrelsome impulses brought by the hostility star.

Two other animal signs enjoying excellent potential are those born in the years of the **Dog** (the Rabbit's secret friend) and the **Boar** (the Rabbit's ally), although for them, success luck can diminish if they are affected by discordant forces in their personal charts or simply have outdated feng shui in the home or they get hit by annual flying stars. The Boar needs to stay updated and be careful not to have their good potential blocked by the year's afflictive energies. They should check to make sure neither their main door nor their bedrooms are afflicted this year.

The **Dragon** has an uneventful year. It should sail through 2011 with small luck. Success is limited, but there is little to cause them grief. For the Dragon, heaven luck shines bright, so there could be unexpected windfalls. It is a good idea to enhance for special luck to manifest. For the Dragon, wearing and displaying **good luck charms** is sure to be beneficial.

The **Sheep**, the Rabbit's ally, benefits from the year, but only when there is an adequate supply of Earth element energy, so this sign needs strengthening with the **Earth Seal**. It also pays to display and wear raw and **natural quartz crystal**.

The **Monkey** has a harder time staying ahead of the competition, especially those working professionally pursuing a career. Those doing business need to be careful not to get conned. This sign could fall victim to external politicking. The Monkey must be wary and alert to false friends and ambitious colleagues. It is beneficial to carry amulets that fight against the evil eye!

Finally, the **Tiger** has to work at generating heaven luck energy by wearing the **Heaven Seal**. Doing so brings good fortune. This is a year when depending on its own instincts benefits them more than listening to others.

HOUR	DAY	MONTH	YEAR
HEAVENLY STEM	HEAVENLY STEM	HEAVENLY STEM	HEAVENLY STEM
壬	庚	庚	辛
YANG WATER	YANG METAL	YANG METAL	YIN METAL
EARTHLY BRANCH	EARTHLY BRANCH	EARTHLY BRANCH	EARTHLY BRANCH
丙午	甲寅	甲寅	乙卯
FIRE HORSE	WOOD TIGER	WOOD TIGER	WOOD RABBIT

HIDDEN HEAVENLY STEMS OF THE YEAR			
YANG FIRE YANG EARTH	YANG FIRE YANG EARTH YANG WOOD	YANG FIRE YANG EARTH YANG WOOD	YIN WOOD

The year is desperately short of EARTH ie Resource

The Year's Four Pillars

The first indicator we look at to get an overall feel for the destiny outlook for the year is the year's Four Pillars chart. This offers a snapshot of the year and reveals the hidden forces that affect the fortunes of the year. To know what's in store, we analyse the eight elements that dominate the four pillars i.e. the heavenly stems and the earthly branches that rule the chi energies of the year.

The preceding Tiger Year was a year of unstable earth disasters characterized by rogue waves in the seas and plenty of big earthquakes that began at the start of the year and continued on unabated through the year... from Chile to Japan to Turkey to Indonesia to China and Taiwan. Last year, hidden Earth energies rumbled and brought tragedy and disaster to many parts of the globe.

In this coming year 2011 of the Golden Metallic Rabbit, its Four Pillars Chart looks rather foreboding. In fact, the chart is indicating not one pillar of directly clashing elements, but FOUR!

Yes, all four of the pillars have discordant crushing energies, with three pillars indicating Metal crushing Wood, instantly telling us that the Rabbit of 2011 is not going to be a docile one. The remaining pillar has Water destroying Fire.

So in 2011, all four pillars that make up the Eight Characters chart of the year are showing direct clashes. This is a nasty indication and it is a clear warning for everyone to be careful and circumspect. Travel and risk-taking are best kept to a minimum, and it is a good idea to be prepared at all times. It is not a year to tempt fate. This is a general but potent piece of advice for the year. Better to stay home than to travel. Better to stay safe than to take risks.

Just glance quickly at the chart and instantly you will see that in the DAY, MONTH and YEAR pillars, Metal is destroying Wood! These are direct clashes and here we see both yin and yang pillars having the same clashing characteristics.

And then in the HOUR pillar, Water is destroying Fire! Each one of the four pillars indicates extremely negative outlooks for the year; so from year start to year end, and affecting all age groups, hostile energies dominate. This has to be a record of some kind; to have all four pillars showing a clash of elements with the heavenly stem elements destroying the earthly branches in every single pillar of the chart.

Disharmony is thus the prominent force of the coming year and despite the Rabbit, usually an icon of diplomacy, it appears that feng shui cosmic forces this year bring plenty of high octane anger and intolerance. In addition, the chart also shows the presence of two Tigers, which suggests that the Tiger energies of 2010 have not entirely abated.

We face a scenario not unlike that of the previous year, but maybe worse; clashing elements are always indicators of hard times, so the energy of the year looks discordant.

The chart shows Metal and Wood dominating, with Metal energy having the upper hand. The essence of the year is Metal, but it is neither weak nor strong Metal. Although we see three Metal, the Water and Fire of the Hour Pillar destroys and weakens the Metal. And because there is no Earth element present in the chart, Metal lacks the resources to stay strong.

There appears then to be a lack of resources during the year, and this is another bad sign. The absence of Earth also suggests an unbalanced chart, which is another indication of turmoil.

With this obvious imbalance, the prevailing attitude during the year is one of unrelenting intolerance. There are three Metals indicating the presence of competitive pressures, but the strength of the Metals cannot be sustained because of the lack of Earth. This indicates that competitive pressures cannot be sustained and it is best to not be pushed into a corner by competitors. Try thinking outside the box instead of combating the competition!

The Good News

When we look at the hidden elements of the chart, the news for 2011 is not all bad. Underlying all the competing energy lies the potential for the creation of much new wealth. There is hidden Earth bringing unexpected resources to fuel growth for the year, and there is also hidden Wood, indicating unexpected wealth. Likewise, there is also hidden Fire, so the year does not lack for managerial capability. The exercise of authority and leadership plays a big role in transforming the cosmic forces in 2011.

Results may not be evident in the year itself, but there is no denying the positive benefits of good leadership. As the Northwest patriarchal sector this year has the number 8, the cosmic forces are aligned to help the patriarchs i.e. the leaders of the planet. So in the trinity of heaven, earth and man, *tien ti ren*, it will be Mankind energy that prevails and delivers success and results.

Herein lies the good news for those who are commercially minded and business motivated. 2011 is a year when prosperity luck is present. There are many direct as well as indirect wealth-making opportunities emerging.

Although what is apparently missing are direct resources, as indicated by the element Earth which is missing from the main chart, there are thankfully three hidden Earth element. This more than makes up for their absence in the main chart. In effect, the chart can now be said to be balanced with the presence of all five elements, when the hidden elements are taken into account.

What *is* in very small supply however is the element of Water, which was completely missing last year.

In 2011, Water represents creativity, intelligence and common sense. Because it is in such short supply, everyone once again continues to benefit from the **Water element**. This is what will create Wood which stands for wealth this year. Water also exhausts Metal which is destroying the Wood element.

Thus the source of wealth creation in 2011 is Water; i.e. creativity - original and strategic thinking which will open the way to mining the year's prosperity. Much of this creativity will come from the younger generation. This will be a year when those who have just joined the workforce, and those who have recently graduated out of school and college will be the source of new ideas. And because it is the year of the Rabbit, when the East sector comes into prominence, it is likely that those born as eldest sons of their families are the ones whose stars shine brightly. The year benefits the eldest sons of families.

Rabbit Years have always been years of appeasement, when conflicts arising in preceding Tiger Years get resolved. Unfortunately, 2011 continues to be a year of global political upheavals.

For the Rabbit-born, there is the wu wang or five yellow to contend with. So despite it being your year, you need to be alert and careful.

But the Golden Rabbit Year is challenging and full of intrigues. Unlike the direct confrontations of the previous year, this is a year when unexpected betrayals and underhand tactics become prevalent. For the Rabbit, it is likely that you will have to contend with quite a fair bit of power play and the key to overcoming bad vibes like these is for you to stay calm and patient. Those feeling this darker side of the year's energy need to have a positive and non-defeatist attitude; only then can the coming twelve months from February 4th 2011 to February 4th 2012 benefit you. Then in spite of discordant element indications, you can create and accumulate new assets.

There is wealth luck in 2011. The Rabbit might however have to give wealth creation a miss this year. Keep an eye out for opportunities and think outside the box, but do this to preserve what you already have rather than to create wealth. The global business scenario is changing fast and you need to adapt. New technology and applications of this fast-developing new technology is racing ahead at breakneck speed.

Globally, there is more than one prominent player in the technology game. Increasingly the world is feeling the presence of China. Note that Period 7 benefitted the West, but it is the **Northeast** that is ruling the energies of the current Period 8. This Period favors China. Both the year 2011 and the Period itself favors those who move fast; have prepared themselves to penetrate uncharted territory, just like water. We borrow the term blue oceans to suggest the clever opening up of new areas for creating wealth. And it does not matter whether you live in the West or in the Northeast, if you can work with the cosmic forces of the year and the period, you are sure to benefit.

Water is Vital

This is once again a year when the Water element brings prosperity, although not in the same way it did in the previous year. Those of you who installed water features last year and benefited from them will benefit again from it.

Note that in 2011, we are seeing three Metal destroying three Wood - i.e. clashing directly. The Metal of the year's heavenly stems continues to destroy the intrinsic Wood of the earthly branches. On the surface, this is not a good sign.

But Metal, when used with skill and under special circumstances, can transform Wood into something of greater value. So even as Metal destroys Wood, it can transform Wood into an object of value.

What is great for this year is that there is more than enough Wood around to make up for whatever gets destroyed. Note from the Pillars chart there are three hidden Wood element, so there is definitely wealth to be created and accumulated.

But clashing elements always suggest hostilities, so the wars of the world will not see any easing or closure. In 2011, fighting continues with little hope for reconciliation; competition in the commercial environment and between companies and countries will get worse. The energies of Heaven and Earth are clashing. So it is left to the energy of Mankind to make up for all the imbalances.

Mankind energy can be harnessed very effectively to overcome the discordant energies of heaven and earth this year. All the resources required are available, the only snag being they are hidden and so, not immediately obvious. But they are there!

Here we can use the third dimension of feng shui - the powerful inner chi dimension - to transform and enhance the space and time chi of 2011 at individual personalized levels. Irrespective of the discordance of Heaven and Earth, those of us who know how can still arrange our lives to benefit from the hidden forces of the year. We can focus on the mankind chi within all of us, concentrate on strengthening it, and in so doing, more effectively harness the spiritual energy of the empowered self to overcome obstacles and emerge triumphant.

There are methods and rituals we can use to subdue negative energies caused by the four sets of clashing elements. We can also apply element therapy to bring about a much improved balance in the elements in our immediate environments; and in addition, there are symbolic cures that are made into amulets and talismans that can subdue the negative "stars".

The Commanding Star

A very positive aspect of the year is the appearance of the *Commanding Star*, which is an outstandingly auspicious star. Its appearance in the 2011 chart is brought about by the presence of the Earthly Branch of Horse in the Hour pillar and the Earthly branch of Tiger in the Day pillar. This excellent indication arises out of the ally relationship that exists between Horse and Tiger. Here the Commanding Star suggests traits brought by these two fearless animal signs to the year. It brings good vibrations benefiting those who show courage and fortitude.

The Commanding Star suggests the presence of authority, power and influence luck for the year, benefiting those who find themselves in a leadership situation or those holding a position of authority. Indeed, the year will benefit those who know how to use their positions of influence and power; so managers and leaders who have a clear idea what their strategy or focus are will benefit from this star - despite the clashing elements of the year.

Leaders will find the energy of the year increases their charisma and their effectiveness. The exercise of authority will come easily. Those born in the years of the Rabbit however have to contend with the affliction of the *wu wang*.

As such you, the Rabbit person must be more aware than ever that to succeed in 2011, you will first need to suppress the misfortune bringing energy of the wu wang. The star number 5 is a dreaded star much feared by those who understand about feng shui afflictions. So for you the advice is to stay low key this year.

What can be worrying about the Commanding Star is that both the elements of the Hour Pillar - Water and Fire - are not good for the intrinsic element of the year. Here we see Fire destroying Metal, and Water exhausting Metal. Superficially then, it appears that the Commanding Star can turn ugly, bringing obstacles instead of opportunities. For the Rabbit who is under the cloud of the wu wang, it is necessary to be careful they do not fall victim the negative effects of the Commanding Star.

Flying Stars of 2011

The feng shui chart of the year which lays out the location of the year's flying stars in 2011 is dominated by the energy of 7, a weak star; but being the reigning number, its effect cannot be overlooked. The number 7 is a Metal number that represents the negative side of relationships, symbolizing duplicity and treachery. The number adds fuel to the discordant vibes of the clashing elements of the Four Pillars.

So even though the Rabbit Year is usually a subdued one, 2011 has its full share of confrontation; global incidence of violence is likely to continue.

This is a year when intrigue and situational upheavals occur frequently; brought by a higher occurrence of betrayals and unbridled ambitions. It is a year when the center of buildings, houses and offices benefit from Water energy to subdue the strength of 7. Luckily, the number 7 is a weak star in the current Period of 8, so it is not difficult to subdue. Anything of a dark blue color is sufficient for keeping it under control.

It is advisable to make the effort to suppress the number 7 in homes and offices. This brings protection for residents and prevents them from falling victim to external politicking and trouble-making people.

SE	SOUTH	SW
SMALL AUSPICIOUS	BIG AUSPICIOUS	EARTH SEAL
6	2	4
SMALL AUSPICIOUS	BIG AUSPICIOUS	ROBBERY STAR
TAI SUI		
5	7	9
FIVE YELLOW		3 KILLINGS
HEAVEN SEAL	BIG AUSPICIOUS	YEARLY CONFLICT
1	3	8
GOLDEN DEITY	BIG AUSPICIOUS	YI DUO STAR
NE	NORTH	NW

EAST / WEST

In 2011 it is a great idea to activate the power of Water in the home. Invest in a small water feature to create a small presence of moving water in the center grid of the home. Or place a Rhino or Elephant there. Together, these three remedies are excellent for suppressing the negative influence of 7.

The luck of the different sectors of any structure is influenced by the new energy brought by the year's feng shui chart, as this reveals the year's lucky and unlucky sectors for buildings, houses and apartments.

The chart for 2011 indicates different numbers in each of the nine grids in this three-by-three sector chart. This looks like the original Lo Su square which plays such a big role in time dimension feng shui except that each year, the numbers placed in each grid change according to the center number. With 7 in the center, the other numbers are then placed around the grid sectors. This is what changes the pattern of energy in homes and offices from year to year.

The numbers play a big part in determining the "*luck outlook*" of animal signs arising from the fact that each of the twelve signs occupies a designated compass location. Thus the Rabbit person occupies the East location and we can see from the chart that Rabbit people come under the cloud of the wu wang, the five yellow, which brings misfortunes. Unfortunately, the wu wang is reflected in the constellation of the 24 mountains.

The stars of the 24 mountains are influential. There are 108 different fortune stars, but only a handful fly into the 24 mountain directions in any year. These bring auspicious or harmful influences, but they vary in strength and type each year. For the Rabbit this year, they are afflictive and must be suppressed to ensure that the year does not sour on you.

Houses and animal signs are affected in the same way by the 24 mountain stars. Some stars bring good luck, some bring misfortune. When your sign is negatively afflicted and your vitality gets weakened, you need to wear specific protective Taoist charms. These protect you from the affliction or they reduce its effects.

We have made different charms to match each animal sign's needs. What you, the Rabbit, need are **strong remedial amulets** that can suppress the wu wang, both to wear and for placement in the East sector of your home. There are also other talismans to attract good fortune. These are highlighted in Section 5 of the book.

But your energy must first be protected; only then can you attract good fortune. The Rabbit's energy is afflicted this year and the 24 Mountain stars are also not helping. Get yourself the required cures and stay strong and healthy this year.

The **Annual Protection Amulet** has been designed to counter afflictions specific to year 2011.

Not many people know that it is essential to be mentally and physically strong to attract good fortune. After making sure that afflictions are suppressed, you can attract good feng shui with powerful symbols of good fortune. But for these to be effective, you must also stay healthy and strong. You must not allow your confidence to get undermined by the five yellow, so stay optimistic and maintain good health through the year.

This is what brings you the yang vigor needed to actualize good fortune. This helps to generate the third dimension to your luck - which is the *empowerment of the self*. It is this that makes the difference between succumbing to bad luck or transforming it into good luck. The process of transformation requires powerful self empowering energy. More on this later.

Staying Updated Each Month

Meanwhile, note that the monthly updates are just as important as the annual ones. Monthly luck forecasts are the highlight of this book because good timing plays an important part in attracting good fortune; and avoiding misfortunes. To enjoy good luck through the year, you must update your month to month feng shui. So you must keep track of how cosmic energies affect your luck each month. Every animal sign can be alerted to the high and low points of their year, and be warned against negative energy. As well as to spur you on during months when your chi energy is high. When to lie low and when to be go bravely forth are important to maximizing the opportunities of the year, so irrespective of whether the year is good or bad, you can avoid pitfalls and not miss out on chances that come your way.

Nothing beats being prepared against potential misfortune because this reduces their impact. Knowing the nature of misfortune - whether it is related to illness, or accident, betrayal or plain bad luck - helps you cope when the misfortune does occur. What is better is that when you wear protective remedies, mantra amulets or talismans, these are very effective in warding off misfortunes.

Thus an important aspect of reading these books is to take note of the spikes and dips in your monthly luck focusing on Career, Business, Family, Love and Study luck. The monthly readings analyze each month's Lo Shu numbers, element, trigram and paht chee luck pillars. These accurately identify your good and bad months; they generate valuable pointers on how to navigate safely and successfully through the year, effectively helping you get your timing right on important decisions and actions.

The recommendations in this book alert you to months when you are vulnerable to illness, accidents or dangers. We also highlight good luck months and this is when exciting new opportunities come to you. Knowing when will give you a competitive edge on timing. You will get better at coping with setbacks and overcoming obstacles that occur from month to month.

Improving Your Luck

Your luck can be substantially improved through the placement of symbolic enhancers or remedies in the spaces you occupy. This is a book on the personalized approach for you to attract good luck. You will see as you delve deeper into it, that there are many ways you can improve your personalized luck despite the year being afflicted for you.

What you need to place in your compass sector changes from year to year. You must be sure what exactly you need to place in your East location in 2011, both to suppress wu wang and also to energize the sector. For the Rabbit, the best way of attracting good fortune is to activate Water for the East sectors of all your main rooms.

Your luck is affected by the year's flying stars (shown in the feng shui chart) as well as the elements of the four pillars and the luck stars of the 24 mountains. How you react to the year's changing energies depend on the strength of your spirit essence and your life force. This year 2011 for all animal signs, both of these important indications stay the same as last year. There is no change to your life force and spiritual strength, so all Rabbit people continue to experience the same energy as last year in these two areas. Only the success potential for everyone has changed. This section of the book has thus been shortened. In its place, we are introducing a new aspect that affects your fortunes.

The extra dimension we address this year is to introduce you to your SKY ANIMAL sign. In addition to your birth year animal sign, your destiny and attitudes are also influenced by your lunar mansion.

This is represented by one of the 28 sky animals that correspond to the 28 days in a typical month. This is your Day Sign and it interacts with your Year Sign to add new dimensions to your compatibility with others, and to your luck outlook each year.

Your Lunar Mansion

This is based on the four great constellations that are the foundation of feng shui - the constellations of the *Green Dragon, Crimson Phoenix, Black Tortoise* and *White Tiger*.

The **Green Dragon** rules the Eastern skies while the **Crimson Phoenix** rules the Southern skies. The **White Tiger** is the Lord of the Western Skies and the **Black Tortoise** oversees the Northern skies. Collectively, they rule over the 28 animals of the sky, each having dominance over 7 of them.

Depending on which of the 28 animals is your Day sign, you are under the influence of (and thus protected by) the Dragon, the Tiger, the Phoenix or the Tortoise. These are termed the constellations of the lunar mansion.

Your Sky Animal brings additional insights to the kind of luck you enjoy in any given year depending on your profession or business. The year 2011 is ruled by the Eastern sign of the Rabbit; and with two Tigers in the Pillars chart, this is a year when the Green Dragon who rules the Eastern Skies is dominant. Those whose Day Sign comes under the mighty Dragon are more likely to benefit from the Dragon. Thus bringing the image of the Dragon into your home would be excellent.

The Dragon was very beneficial last year and continues to be the celestial creature that brings good fortune to the year 2011. And since the Water element continues to be in short supply, it is as beneficial to have water and Dragon together, especially in the East sector of your house where it enhances the Rabbit Year, working with the Tiger presence in the Pillars chart to create the Zodiac trinity combination of Spring.

The wearing of any kind of crystal or crystal embossed with Dragon or any kind of Dragon jewellery is especially beneficial in 2011. Everyone will benefit from wearing big chunky natural quartz crystals in 2011 as this signifies the grounding Earth element that is missing from the Pillars chart.

Earth is what provides the year's resources. It strengthens the intrinsic element of the Dragon to balance the double Tiger hence transforming the year's Tiger energy to work powerfully in your favor.

Earth also combines with the Tiger to strengthen the Rabbit energy of the year. This helps to defuse the ferocity of the clashing elements at an individualized level.

Determining your lunar mansion Day Animal requires access to specific calculations retrieved from the Chinese Almanac. In this book, these calculations have been simplified, and any one can quite easily work out their Day Animal sign from the chapter on your lunar mansion. These offer additional insights into your luck outlook for the year.

Updating Your Feng Shui

Buildings are affected by new energy patterns each year. Knowing how to work with these new energies is the key to unlocking good fortune in each new year.

It is important to place remedial updates that safeguard your home and office. This aspect of feng shui is its time dimension and because energy transforms at the start of the year, changing on the day of Spring popularly referred to as the lap chun, it is beneficial for all updates to be put in place before this date which falls on February 4th, 2011.

This corresponds to the start of the solar year of the Chinese Hsia calendar.

Remedial cures are always necessary to subdue the effects of negative stars and malicious influences of bad luck numbers in the flying star chart. The location and strength of these negative influences change from year to year, so it is necessary to check them every year.

Three Dimensions in Feng Shui

Feng shui has three dimensions to its practice, a space, time and self-empowering dimension. These address heaven, earth and mankind chi that make up the trinity of luck that collectively account for how luck works for or against us. If you want to benefit from total feng shui, you should use the collective power of all three dimensions.

Space dimension is governed by environmental feng shui methods - collectively practiced under the broad umbrella of what everyone terms feng shui. Here, it comprises the art of living in harmony with natural landforms and the art of placing auspicious objects with great symbolic meaning and element properties around us. Environmental feng shui takes note of compass directions on a personalized basis and use other methods that focus on lucky and unlucky sectors. Broadly speaking, it takes care of the Earth aspect in the trinity of luck.

Then there is time dimension feng shui, which takes account of changing and transformational energies. This is founded on the premise that energy is never still; that it is constantly changing, and therefore we must see how energy transforms over overlapping cycles of time; annually, monthly, daily, hourly and even in larger time frames that last 20 years, 60 years and 180 years, which is the time it takes for a full nine period cycle of 20 years to complete. In this book, we focus on the all-important annual cycles of change, but we also look at the monthly cycles; and we write this book within the larger context of the Period of 8 cycle. Broadly speaking, time feng shui takes care of the *heavenly* cosmic forces that affect the trinity of luck.

Finally, there is the self or spiritual dimension, which broadly speaking depends on the energies generated by *Mankind*. This focuses on the chi energy individually and collectively created by people themselves. How we each individually, and together with others who live with us, empower the energy of self to either create good or bad energy in our living and work space.

In its highest form, the Self energy is believed to be the most powerful of all, and in the face even of extremely challenging **Heaven Luck** as is the case in

2011, the highly empowered self or highly focused person who has the ability to use the powerful forces of his/her mental concentration can indeed generate the all-powerful **Mankind** chi that can subdue afflictions brought by the intangible conflicting energy of the year's forces (**Heaven Luck**) as well as tangible bad energy caused by bad feng shui (**Earth Luck**).

The highly empowered self does not just happen; this too requires learning, practice and experience, and it involves developing a strongly focused and concentrated mind that can itself generate powerful chi. This is spiritual chi that take years to develop, but there are methods - both gross and subtle - that can be used to generate powerful mankind luck.

These methods are referred to as *inner feng shui*. Traditional feng shui masters of the old school are great adepts at invoking the Taoist spiritual deities through meditative contemplations, reciting powerful prayers and mantras and using purification rituals to remove obstacles.

Many turn to Buddhist deities who are believed to be very powerful in helping to awaken the inner forces within us.

A great deal of feng shui history is thus tied up with Taoism and Buddhist practices in ancient China.

However, this aspect of feng shui is usually kept secret by the Masters, many of whom are also expert at meditation techniques. It is meditation that enables them to access their highly empowered inner chi which brings their practice of feng shui to a much higher level of accomplishment.

We found that many of the powerful ancient rituals for overcoming life obstacles such as those using incense and aromas and the empowering of symbolic and holy objects to enhance the spiritual energy of homes found their way to Tibet during the Tang dynasty, where they were incorporated into their spiritual practices, especially those practices that invoked the powerful Protectors of the Land of Snows. These rituals are now being revealed to the world by the high lamas of Tibetan Buddhism.

In 2011, it will be especially effective to practice this method of feng shui, as it will alleviate many of the discordant energies of the coming year.

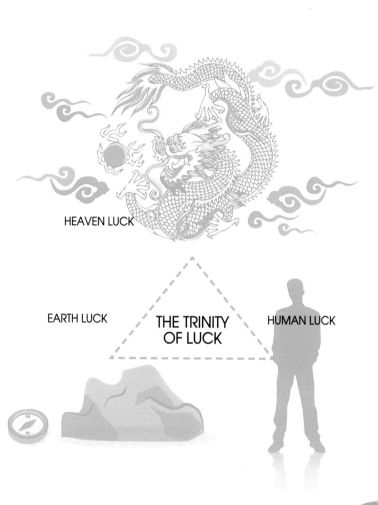

HEAVEN LUCK

EARTH LUCK

THE TRINITY OF LUCK

HUMAN LUCK

Rabbit's Resilience Jumpstarts Luck In 2011

Part 2

- Metal Rabbit – 60 years
- Water Rabbit – 48 years
- Wood Rabbit – 36 years
- Fire Rabbit – 24 years
- Earth Rabbit – 12 years

Outlook for the Rabbit In 2011

The Rabbit sign has to steel itself against some feng shui afflictions in 2011, the most serious of which is the wu wang or five yellow, a cosmic ailment which attracts hardships and negative outcomes, obstacles and illness. This is one of the more feared of the annual afflictions, and this is why it is relatively easier to deal with.

Powerful remedies are available to reduce the effect and impact of *wu wang* simply because Feng Shui practitioners have always been mindful of the woes brought by this condition. Its effect affects different signs in different years and the severity of its impact also differs from year to year. In 2011, thankfully for the Rabbit, the wu wang, which is an Earth element affliction, has its strength reduced by the strong Wood energy of the East location.

Despite this, Rabbit-born people must make certain they do not cause too much disturbance in their own East location. With the wu wang there, excessive noise caused by knocking, banging, renovations and moving house is sure to activate its negative effects, which then manifest as obstacles and misfortune. Sometimes the wu wang can also cause accidents and illness. The secret to keeping it harmless is to suppress it with powerful remedies and also ensure it stays dormant by not energizing it.

The Rabbit needs the **five element pagoda** and the **crystal water globe**, both strengthened by the **tree of life**; using these symbolic cures and therefore updating the Rabbit's annual feng shui should bring the resilience needed to protect itself from the wu wang while simultaneously jump-starting good luck for the year. These two remedies should protect the Rabbit against some pretty nasty hindrances.

These can be rather overwhelming in 2011. Although the Rabbit dominates the year, it is confronted by some dire challenges. The gusts of strongly negative feng shui winds are blowing quite strong in the East this year. Apart from the wu wang, the Rabbit must also face the *Three Killings* and the *Natural Disaster* star sending shards of sharp edgy energy from the West!

Not only does the West house the Rabbit's astrological enemy the Rooster, but it is also where three very unfriendly stars of the 24 mountains constellation are sitting, taking aim at the Rabbit. These, when combined with the decline of its success chi in its horoscope chart, make 2011 something of a challenging year for the mild-mannered and gentle Rabbit.

The good news is that the *Tai Sui* or Lord of the Year is backing the Rabbit which brings good support. The Tai Sui can enhance Rabbit's life force and spiritual inner energies, as such bringing better balance to Rabbit's energy situation for the year.

The Rabbit has always been diplomatic and stoic; and its advantage is its ability to lie low, digging deep into the ground to safeguard itself from the gusts of negative winds. It is not a provocative sign and when confronted by negativity the first instinct is to take flight. For those who fight their fears and confront the situation however, the year's energies can be transformed.

Despite the afflictions of the year for instance, the 48 year old **Water Rabbit** benefits very much from its heavenly stem of water, so this Rabbit will experience financial gains this year. Economic luck is good, in fact excellent, as money flows in quite effortlessly. In 2011, all signs with Water in their heavenly stems, like the Water Rabbit, experience very good wealth luck.

But the Rabbit sign especially benefits from Water energy, being a Wood element sign and being located in the East, a Wood sector; hence you can enhance your money luck very considerably by installing water features in the East side of your garden or by putting an indoor water feature by the East wall of your living room. The presence of the Water element anywhere in your home, but especially in the East sectors of your rooms, is what will bring enhancement to every Rabbit's luck in 2011.

The younger **Fire Rabbit** also enjoys good money and health luck. At 24 years of age, you could yet transform an otherwise difficult year to your advantage. What you also need is to use water as a feng shui enhancer for your East corners. This should help you in any kind of transformational activity you undertake, such as changing your place of work, moving to another residence, making a commitment to someone such as getting engaged or married, or relocating for a change of environment. Any kind of big decision you make this year will be transformative by virtue of your age, and how they eventually turn out for you depends as much on luck as on good timing.

Money should not become a problem in any change made, so it is beneficial to make its flow in your life stable and consistent. Your horoscope helps you, but the cosmic winds of the year do not, so it is advisable to be careful. Think carefully.

Money luck for the 60 year old **Metal Rabbit** is low and for 36 year old **Wood Rabbit** is dismal. It is likely that whatever auspicious luck comes to you will not be in improved net worth. You could even both be looking at a net loss for the year. If you can overcome the obstacles in your way, it should be counted as a meaningful personal triumph. Generally then, the outlook for all Rabbits is that the year holds out some very valuable learning experiences. Obstacles are certain to appear, but in overcoming them comes some pretty positive and far reaching realizations that will strengthen you.

Look on whatever misfortune befall you this year as purification, as the passing of some bad karma. Taking this attitude will lessen the long term impact of any bad experience. Remember also that sometimes good things can come wrapped in unattractive packaging. Stay upbeat and the year will seem to fly past faster than you expect.

The Rabbit Personality in 2011

The Rabbit sign is assailed by some despondency this year so it will be understandable if you tend to be lacking in good humor this year, but the rest and good energy experienced in the previous year should help you retain your generally amiable disposition. But it is hard to expect the Rabbit to be as cheerful or as smiling in view of the challenges of the year.

However, you will continue to maintain your quiet air of confidence and this is because your calm demeanour arises from your positive spirit essence. So internally and spiritually, you will be strong, and this alone will help you to pierce through some of the tougher months. It will also be a busy year for you as there are many things happening all at the same time. Work and domestic concerns demand your attention. But you will also find that you have never felt so good. The harder the challenges confronting you, the better you will perform. By the middle of the year in July, you will have mastered the art of juggling chores and coping when a hundred different things are demanding your attention.

It is an excellent indication that 2011 has the lap chun - what the Chinese refer to as the start of Spring. The Rabbit is the main representative of this important season when fresh new growth takes place. In this month, the Rabbit enjoys luck from heaven, so cosmic forces are on your side this month, so at least the start of the year will be auspicious for you. It is the month of March that you need to pay attention to the double wu wang energy. Hopefully by then, your remedies against this affliction will have been put in place.

The Rabbit should take advantage of the positive months of the year - getting your timing right and adjusting your decisions to the optimum timing will do wonders for you in 2011. You have a natural ability to network effectively; besides, your pleasant disposition ensures that you can naturally borrow the luck of allies and secret friend. Socially, your popularity with colleagues and co-workers is not expected to decline in any way. This should help you in a difficult year. Networking will bring you significant professional successes in your year because you get the support of influential people, from the start of the new year in February and also in September... for Water and Fire Rabbits there can also be promotion of some kind.

OUTLOOK FOR
THE LADY RABBIT IN 2011

BIRTH YEAR	TYPE OF RABBIT LADY	LO SHU AT BIRTH	AGE	LUCK OUTLOOK IN 2011
1951	Metal Rabbit Lady	4	60	Advisable to take it easy this year
1963	Water Rabbit Lady	1	48	Brilliant wealth-making luck
1975	Wood Rabbit Lady	7	36	Feeling short of money
1987	Fire Rabbit Lady	4	24	Strongly forging ahead
1999	Earth Rabbit Girl	1	12	Pacing yourself brings better results

The Lady Rabbit in 2011 continues to feel on top of the world in 2011 despite some afflictions which bring setbacks and reduces the high energy successes of last year. But you should not lose the momentum generated by last year's good fortune luck, because in 2011, you will need all your social and networking skills to negotiate some of the more trying tribulations of the year. But with a positive inner chi strength, you will maintain your composure through the year.

The female Rabbit exudes a restful charm that enables her to benefit from her astrological allies (the Boar and the Sheep) and her secret friend (the Dog) all of whom are looking at a stronger year than her. She will be effective at getting their cooperation and obtaining their support - and this will make a difference not just to her luck, but more importantly, also to her moods and her personality.

It is really necessary to maintain good humor and not allow the aggravations of the year get you down. As in the previous year, **Fire** and **Water Rabbits** will be the most forthcoming and optimistic in 2011, although the Rabbit lady is generally popular and has the skill to create an active circle of friends around her. Rabbit women will take on new challenges, getting involved in community work and charitable projects that broaden their horizons socially, if they have not already done so last year.

Professionally, however, success luck is in short supply but this will not pose too severe a discouraging factor. If you make a strong effort to stay upbeat, take note of difficult months and keep your feng shui updated. The year should move along more quickly than you realise. During the months of **March** and **December**, it might be useful to consider learning how to appease bad feng shui winds by using incense rituals. This is really effective for overcoming obstacles and setbacks, especially when you use specially-formulated naga incense, a blend of powerful mountain herbs produced according to powerful lineage formulas by some of the Tibetan Buddhist style monasteries of Katmandu in Nepal.

Burning incense can dissipate bad feng shui
winds that may blow your way.

OUTLOOK FOR THE GENTLEMAN RABBIT IN 2011

BIRTH YEAR	TYPE OF RABBIT MAN	LO SHU AT BIRTH	AGE	LUCK OUTLOOK IN 2011
1951	Metal Rabbit Man	4	60	Do not overly stress yourself
1963	Water Rabbit Man	1	48	Financially very strong
1975	Wood Rabbit Man	7	36	Keep watch over your finances
1987	Fire Rabbit Man	4	24	Stay optimistic & alert
1999	Earth Rabbit Boy	1	12	Go for steady pregress

The gentleman Rabbit has to confront some difficulties in 2011 but despite this rises admirably to the occasion. This generally mild-mannered and accommodating fellow has plenty of friends who help him negotiate through the mine field of afflictions hurting the Rabbit's location in 2011. Misfortune winds blow in the Rabbit's direction requiring him to stay calm and maintain his equipoise. This proves harder for the male than the female as his networking skills are not as good as that of his female counterpart.

But the Male Rabbit also finds it more strenuous to stay upbeat. So the year tends to be more difficult for him than for her.

The Rabbit man however is just as good at keeping friends, being warm and sensitive and he is rarely if ever offensive. They are sensitive to the feelings of others even when they do not have to be, so that people have time for them and should they need to lean on them, friends will always be supportive and there are always strong shoulders available. This is one of the intrinsic built-in luck characteristics of the Rabbit person. They have what the Chinese refer to as "*people luck*".

In 2011, the Rabbit man is likely to find both the Boar and the Dog especially helpful as they are "*friends*" he can count on. The two most successful and confident men this year will be 49 year old **Water Rabbit** and the 24 year old **Fire Rabbit** – the man in the prime of his career and the young man about to set out on a career. Both will enjoy success luck and there is also prosperity luck.

Health-wise, the year should also pan out well - and this in spite of the wu wang affliction and the confrontation with the three killings star.

The other gentlemen Rabbits may not share the financial luck of their Water and Fire counterparts, but they should also be doing as well if they can install water features in the East sector of their garden.

Rabbit-born are advised to install a **yang water feature** in the East sector of the garden...

Personal Horoscope Luck in 2011

The Rabbit's Life Force luck is showing a single cross, X which indicates some small but hidden danger in 2011. This luck category usually reveals hidden threats to your life that pose the threat of premature death, or cause suffering over a period of time.

When the year shows a higher incidence of natural disasters such as last year's earthquakes and volcanic activity around the world, it is advisable to take this warning seriously and to make sure you are protected during the current year, especially since Rabbit also faces the *Natural Disaster* star in the West.

Natural calamities bring havoc and they occur without warning. This year's paht chee chart suggests that the world continues to be under a cloud of conflicting energy patterns. As such, the single X in Rabbit's horoscope suggests you need to be protected by sacred talismans that incorporate powerful holy syllables and mantras. Wearing or carrying these is an easy and accessible way to evade danger threats to you and your family. Meanwhile, doing something good for charity strengthens the power of the protection, because then, whatever danger may be coming to your physical person will be efficiently averted. Threats to one's Life Force usually represents the karmic ripening of some non-virtuous behaviour on your part in this or some past life, and can be purified by acts of kindness in this lifetime. It is a good idea to be alert to the opportunity to help someone if you can.

Meanwhile, the Rabbit's Spirit Essence is one circle O and this is regarded as a very positive indication, especially when viewed against the unfavorable and negative wu wang in your location. This category of luck is more important and vital than other categories. It reveals the strength of your inner resilience and spiritual strength in any year. When your inner essence is strong, you do not feel fear or experience nervousness in the face of hardship or adversity. It also means a lower susceptibility to spiritual afflictions, and a greater effectiveness in overcoming negative showings in other categories of luck. Circles suggest an inner calm and one O also indicates you are blessed. You will find it easy to be strongly positive; and what's better is that you can pull out of any bad luck situation.

In terms of Health/Finance/Success luck, this differs for each of the Rabbit persons categorised according to age and the element of their heavenly stem. The luck ratings of everyone born in the Rabbit year are shown in the tables below. These give a meaningful snapshot of your personal horoscope luck for year 2011.

Luck in 2011
Earth Rabbit - 72 & 12 Years Old

TYPE OF LUCK	ELEMENT AT BIRTH AFFECTING THIS LUCK	ELEMENT IN 2011 AFFECTING THIS LUCK	LUCK RATING
LIFE FORCE	Wood	Wood	X
HEALTH LUCK	Earth	Wood	XX
FINANCE LUCK	Earth	Metal	OX
SUCCESS LUCK	Fire	Fire	X
SPIRIT ESSENCE	Water	Water	0

HEALTH LUCK - showing XX indicates disturbing health ailments.

FINANCE LUCK - showing OX means there is no discernible improvement in your economic status.

SUCCESS LUCK - showing X - big decline from last year. Some setbacks to your luck this year.

Luck in 2011
Metal Rabbit - 60 Years Old

TYPE OF LUCK	ELEMENT AT BIRTH AFFECTING THIS LUCK	ELEMENT IN 2011 AFFECTING THIS LUCK	LUCK RATING
LIFE FORCE	Wood	Wood	X
HEALTH LUCK	Wood	Wood	X
FINANCE LUCK	Metal	Metal	X
SUCCESS LUCK	Fire	Fire	X
SPIRIT ESSENCE	Water	Water	0

HEALTH LUCK - showing X indicates minor health ailments with the occasional bout of flu or muscular ache.

FINANCE LUCK - showing X means you could sustain a minor loss this year.

SUCCESS LUCK - showing X - big decline from last year. Some setbacks to your luck this year.

Luck in 2011
Water Rabbit - 48 Years Old

TYPE OF LUCK	ELEMENT AT BIRTH AFFECTING THIS LUCK	ELEMENT IN 2011 AFFECTING THIS LUCK	LUCK RATING
LIFE FORCE	Wood	Wood	X
HEALTH LUCK	Metal	Wood	OO
FINANCE LUCK	Water	Metal	OOO
SUCCESS LUCK	Fire	Fire	X
SPIRIT ESSENCE	Water	Water	O

HEALTH LUCK - showing OO means you are in good health with no problems this year.

FINANCE LUCK - showing OOO means you enjoy a super year in terms of financial improvements.

SUCCESS LUCK - showing X - big decline from last year. Some setbacks to your luck this year.

Luck in 2011
Wood Rabbit - 36 Years Old

TYPE OF LUCK	ELEMENT AT BIRTH AFFECTING THIS LUCK	ELEMENT IN 2011 AFFECTING THIS LUCK	LUCK RATING
LIFE FORCE	Wood	Wood	X
HEALTH LUCK	Water	Wood	OX
FINANCE LUCK	Wood	Metal	XX
SUCCESS LUCK	Fire	Fire	X
SPIRIT ESSENCE	Water	Water	0

HEALTH LUCK - showing OX suggests average health luck.

FINANCE LUCK - showing XX means your financial net worth could decline this year.

SUCCESS LUCK - showing X - big decline from last year. Some setbacks to your luck this year.

Luck in 2011
Fire Rabbit - 24 Years Old

TYPE OF LUCK	ELEMENT AT BIRTH AFFECTING THIS LUCK	ELEMENT IN 2011 AFFECTING THIS LUCK	LUCK RATING
LIFE FORCE	Wood	Wood	X
HEALTH LUCK	Fire	Wood	OOO
FINANCE LUCK	Fire	Metal	OO
SUCCESS LUCK	Fire	Fire	X
SPIRIT ESSENCE	Water	Water	O

HEALTH LUCK - showing OOO suggests excellent health.

FINANCE LUCK - showing OO indicating good financial luck with increase in net worth possible.

SUCCESS LUCK - showing X - big decline from last year. Some setbacks to your luck this year.

Discovering Your Lunar Mansion

How Your Sky Animal Affects Your Luck

Your Lunar Mansion is named one of 28 Sky animals that pinpoint the Day of the week that is favorable for you and more importantly it reveals what sky constellation you belong to thereby opening up a mine of information as to the kind of people you work best with; the area of work that offers the best potential for success; and the nature of the assistance your Sky Animal brings you in any given year. Your Lunar Mansion is an integral part of you so it deepens your understanding of what makes you tick, how it modifies the attitude tendencies and outlook for your Zodiac sign.

DISCOVERING YOUR LUNAR MANSION

How Your Sky Animal Affects Your Luck

There are **four Sky Constellations** under each of which are seven Sky Animals, three of them primary and four, secondary. Those of you born in a Rabbit year will work well with Sky Animals belonging to the Eastern Skies and as a team or partnership they attract good business luck. At the same time your own Sky animal will likewise determine which of other Sky animals work well with you. Basically these are colleagues belonging to the same constellation as you. Each constellation refers to one of four sections of the Skies, and these are associated with the four celestial guardians, the Green Dragon, who guards the Eastern skies, the Crimson Phoenix, who protects the Southern Skies, the Black Tortoise, lord of the Northern Skies, and the White Tiger, who rules the Western Skies.

The Celestials and the Sky Animals mirror the celestial guardians of feng shui and the Zodiac animal signs that make up the earthly branches of Astrology. This mirror effect strengthens specific types of good fortune. Sky Animals rarely bring obstacles as their effect is generally positive. They signify the influence of heaven.

Lucky Day

Everyone is born on a DAY that corresponds to one of these Sky Animals. In astrological terms, this is the lucky DAY for you. It is described as your corresponding lunar mansion and it reveals the influence of star constellations on your professional and business life from year to year. One's lunar mansion is analyzed in conjunction with one's personal Four Pillars chart and the Four Pillars chart of the year. Such a detailed analysis is not within the scope of this book, but it is useful to know the trends brought by the influence of your lunar mansion (or Sky Animal) in terms of your relationships and your luck in 2011.

Compatibility

For instance, everyone belonging to the same constellation and coming under the same Celestial Guardian has an affinity with each other, and in times of trouble, one can depend on the other, sometimes even in spite of them being opposing signs based on year of birth.

Sky animals also have natural affinity to their corresponding Zodiac animal signs e.g. a Sky Rabbit has affinity with someone born in the year of the Rabbit and vice versa and Sky Rabbit also have affinity with someone born in the year of the Boar or Sheep (Rabbit's allies). This applies for all 12 animal Zodiac signs as each sign has a Sky counterpart!

Meanwhile, you can also be a secret friend of a Sky animal. Thus the Sky Dog is the secret friend of the Rabbit. This creates very powerful work luck as your heaven and earth chi blend well. This is a heaven and earth relationship. In itself, this is an indication of auspicious chi, so it is good for the Rabbit to go into partnership with someone who is a Sky Dog.

Determining the Dominant Celestial Guardian

The coming year 2011 is a Rabbit Year with two Tigers and a Horse in its Pillars chart. This suggests that the Green Dragon who rules the Eastern Skies is dominant. This arises from it being a Rabbit Year and the Rabbit is one of the Sky signs belonging to the Dragon constellation.

The Dragon rules the Skies of the East and included in this constellation is also the Sky Tiger. The Zodiac

Tiger whose location is part of the East also makes appearances in the year's paht chee.

The strength and influence of the Dragon's constellation is thus very powerful in 2011. It is definitely beneficial to invite the image of the Dragon into the home in 2011.

Note especially that in 2011, the lunar year begins on the **3rd of February** which corresponds to the day before the lap chun, the day of Spring. This is an auspicious indication. This could bring miracles to the year and help in transforming conflict energy into something productive.

With the Dragon as the ruling celestial guardian, growth energy during the year will be strong. The Sky Dragon is the key to subduing all discordant energies brought by the clashing elements on earth. Lining up all seven animals of the Dragon's constellation is believed to bring greater strength for getting projects started and attracting the good fortune of the Sky Dragon constellation. This applies to the Rabbit, its seasonal ally, the Dragon, as well as to those born in the sign of the Tiger.

Even just placing the three main Sky signs of this constellation - the Dragon, Tiger and Rabbit -would be extremely auspicious and it benefits to place them in the East part of your garden or along an East wall of your living room. Sky signs look exactly like their Zodiac counterparts.

Green Dragon Constellation

The seven Sky animals that belong to the Dragon's constellation of the Eastern skies are the Sky Dragon, Sky Rabbit and Sky Tiger as well as the Sky Salamander, Sky Beaver, Sky Fox and Sky Leopard.

1. The Sky Salamander

This sky creature epitomizes the phenomenon of growth energy, associated mainly with agriculture and plantations. Any kind of profession associated with plants, gardens or plantations would be beneficial. This creature is a cousin of the Dragon. Rabbit people with this sign can rely on their creative instincts. You have good fortune in 2011 and your heaven luck is good. Your lucky day is Thursday.

2. The Sky Dragon

This powerful creature is said to be a magician, able to create wondrous things out of nothing more than dreams. Success comes early in life and you could peak earlier than you wish. The Rabbit born with this sign find their forte in pursuing their own ideas; believing in themselves and moving bravely forward. Be courageous this year and there could big things coming your way in 2011. Stay relaxed! Your lucky day is Friday.

3. The Sky Beaver

This is a creature that signifies stability and good foundation. If this is your sign, you should seek out mentors, people senior to you who could bring you "follow my leader luck". A abbit born with this Sky Animal sign usually benefits enormously because the Sky Beaver enhances the Rabbit's networking luck, which will open pathways to many lucrative opportunities. Your lucky day is Saturday.

4. The Sky Rabbit

This is the most accommodating creature of this Constellation, usually associated with bringing family members together and establishing the bliss of domestic comforts. A Rabbit born with this sign will put family above work in 2011. Your lucky day is Sunday.

5. The Sky Fox

This crafty, alert and quick-witted creature complements the character of the amiable and accommodating Rabbit personality. Described as the heart and soul of the Dragon constellation, this creature can steer you to a high position and great success. An asset to any of the twelve signs of the Zodiac. Your lucky day is Monday.

6. The Sky Tiger

This is the creature is said to be born with a jade pendant on its forehead; so power and authority comes naturally to anyone who is a Sky Tiger. Success can be assured in the political arena and they also receive unexpected windfalls of luck all through their life, attracting help and support from family and friends. This lunar mansion benefits the Rabbit-born, bringing some special development for you in 2011. Your lucky day is Tuesday.

7. The Sky Leopard

This is the creature that benefits from being close to the Dragon; the wind beneath the sails, the faithful second in command. Sky leopards are almost always surrounded by many of the good things in life whether or not these belong to them. Nevertheless they are able to enjoy life's luxuries. The Rabbit born as a Sky Leopard can achieve great success if they are discreet, loyal and keep their own counsel. Your lucky day is Wednesday.

Black Tortoise Constellation

For the Rabbit-born, if your Sky Animal comes under the Tortoise constellation, you personify the good life with little effort. This creates complementing energies which make it easier for you to take the fullest advantage of your good fortune indications in 2011. It becomes a double bonus this year.

The animals of the Tortoise Constellation are the Sky Ox (Northeast 1), the Sky Rat (North), and the Sky Boar (Northwest 3). There are also the Sky Unicorn, the Sky Bat, the Sky Swallow and the Sky Porcupine.

8. The Sky Unicorn

This creature combines the speed of the Horse with the courage of the Dragon. For the RABBIT if this is your Sky Animal, it indicates two extreme sides of you, for the Unicorn is at once your best friend and your own worst enemy. Rabbit-born people whose Sky counterpart is the Unicorn could have an exaggerated sense of do-goodness about them. You have to look beyond small grievances and take the big picture approach to attaining all your dreams. Make sure you do not lose out on the main chance. Your lucky day is Thursday.

9. The Sky Ox

This creature is associated with the legend of the weaving maiden and the Ox boy forced to live apart and able to meet only once a year. Rabbit-born people whose Sky Animal is the Ox can borrow Ox's extremely favorable luck in 2011, especially in real estate investments. The single Rabbit could also find true love this year but there might be small obstacles. Your lucky day is Friday.

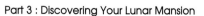

10. The Sky Bat

This is a secondary sign of the Tortoise constellation but it is a symbol that signifies extreme good fortune. Benefits keep coming to you, especially if you are in the construction or engineering profession. Rabbit-born with this Sky sign enjoy a life of comfort, living in a mansion through adult life. The Bat is greatly blessed if living in a temple or turns spiritual. There is good fortune awaiting you in 2011. Your lucky day is Saturday.

11. The Sky Rat

This sign signifies winter where yin energy rules. The Rabbit whose Sky sign is the Sky Rat enjoy auspicious luck brought by 2011. A very auspicious year awaits you. You will be on the receiving end of some good fortune. Your lucky day is Sunday.

12. The Sky Swallow

This is the sign often associated with foolhardiness and danger as the swallow flies too fast and too high. This is the risk taker of the Tortoise constellation and Rabbit-born people having this Sky sign could be a little too impulsive, and as a result could rush into making ill-advised decisions. If this is your sign, it would be advantageous to reflect carefully before committing to anything new. Your lucky day is Monday.

13. The Sky Boar

This is a sign associated with the good life, which gets better as you get older. Rabbit born having this Sky sign are sure to be living in a mansion. You will enjoy good fortune in 2011 and the older you are, the better the luck coming your way. Good year to move into a bigger house. Your lucky day is Tuesday.

14. The Sky Porcupine

This is the policeman of this constellation, always conscious of security, alert to people with dishonest intentions. Rabbit born people having this sign are artistic, hardworking and very committed to what they do. This is a year when you can excel. Do not lose confidence in yourself in 2011, otherwise you might not have the courage to accept what comes your way. Your lucky day is Wednesday.

White Tiger Constellation

The White Tiger constellation tends to be vulnerable in 2011, hence those born into this grouping are advised to take things easy and lie low. The Mountain Stars affecting the Western skies are potentially disastrous, bringing misfortune. Taking risks could be dangerous and the year itself is already showing several warning signs, so it is best not to be too adventurous or foolhardy. Rabbit born people whose Sky Animal falls under this constellation should be alert to warning signs; it is beneficial to take the conciliatory approach at all times. Also, discretion is the better part of valor and it is better to be safe than sorry. This is not a good year for these Sky Animals to be too adventurous. But being an Rabbit born, your year influence will protect you in a positive way.

The Tiger's constellation has the Sky Dog (Northwest 1), the Sky Rooster (West) and the Sky Monkey (Southwest 3). On a compass you can see this reflects the Western skies sector. These are creatures of Autumn, when others are preparing to hibernate. In 2011, when the year is dangerous for this grouping of Sky Animals, it is a good time to stay less active.

The secondary Sky Animals of the Tiger Constellation - the Sky Wolf, Sky Pheasant, Sky Raven and Sky

Ape, protect and support the main creatures with all seven coming under the care of the White Tiger. In astrological terms, the signs in the grouping of the Western Sky creatures are the most commercially-minded of all the Sky Animals. In 2011, protection is the keyword for those belonging to this constellation.

15. The Sky Wolf

This is an insecure creature with a tendency towards negativity, expecting the worse to happen. The Sky Wolf requires plenty of reassurance and it is this lack of confidence that is its worst drawback. A Rabbit who is a Sky Wolf must exert greater efforts to be upbeat especially in 2011. Confidence is the key to succeeding. Your lucky day is Thursday.

16. The Sky Dog

This is an excellent sky sign as it indicates a life of success. The Sky Dog always has a pile of treasures at its feet; commercial and business success comes easily and effortlessly and theirs is a life filled with celebration and merry making. The Rabbit who is also a Sky Dog is sure to find great success in 2011, benefiting from the stars of Big Auspicious. Just remember to be careful this year. Your lucky day is Friday.

17. The Sky Pheasant
This is another extremely good Sky sign as the Pheasant indicates someone successful at creating and keeping their wealth. This is a Sky sign that is particularly suited to a career involving finance such as banking. This sign will also never be short of money as the Sky Pheasant attracts wealth continuously. The Rabbit born with this sign is sure to be rich but do be alert to anyone trying to con you of your money! Your lucky day is Saturday.

18. The Sky Rooster
This creature reflects its Zodiac counterpart, being naturally vigilant and watchful. The Sky Rooster is described as the eyes and ears of the skies, ever alert to those who would disturb the natural order. You are an excellent one to have around in 2011, which is a year when your instincts are at their most alert. Rabbit born with this Sky sign suffer from

their own conflicting judgment calls; you will be going through risky but potentially prosperous times. Your lucky day is Sunday.

19. The Sky Raven

This is the creature of the Sky that signifies extremely rich rewards from efforts expended. The Sky Raven is associated with success of the most outstanding kind. As long as you are determined enough, you will get what you work for. Rabbit born with this sign need to work hard to enjoy a fruitful year in 2011. Your lucky day is Monday.

20. The Sky Monkey

This is a natural born leader who assumes leadership responsibilities without hesitation, naturally extending protective arms outwards. They are thus charismatic and attractive. A Rabbit born under the sign of the Sky Monkey will be a role model of some kind. Others are inspired by you. Your lucky day is Tuesday.

21. The Sky Ape

This is the creature that signifies the important law of karma, ripening for them faster than for others. Thus Sky Ape succeed when they work and find life difficult when they slack off. Good deeds bring instant good rewards and likewise also vile deeds. A Rabbit with this Sky sign will do averagely well in 2011. Your lucky day is Wednesday.

Crimson Phoenix Constellation

The Crimson Phoenix rules the Southern skies and its Sky Animals are the Sky Horse (South), Sky Sheep (Southwest 1), and Sky Snake (Southeast 3). As with the creatures of the other constellations, any family or business entity represented by this group of Sky Animals under the Phoenix benefit each other immensely. Collectively they attract exciting opportunities; their best time comes during the summer months and working on weekends benefits them. The Sky Animals or lunar mansions of the Southern skies are the:

22. The Sky Anteater:

This is a creature that has the potential to exert great influence, but whether or not this can materialize depends on other factors. The Sky Anteater can be a catalyst, but it cannot initiate or spearhead a project or be a leader. But as someone supporting someone else, there is no better person. The Rabbit born with this Sky sign works well behind the scenes. Your lucky day is Thursday.

23. The Sky Sheep

This Sky sign indicates someone who will eventually become deeply spiritual or psychic. When developed to its fullest potential, such a person becomes incredibly charismatic - easily becoming an iconic source of inspiration to others. Rabbits born with this Sky sign have the potential to achieve brilliance as industry leaders or politicians. Your lucky day is Friday.

24. The Sky Roebuck

This is a creature of healing, someone who has the gift to mend broken hearts and emotionally distraught people. Those with this Sky sign have calm dispositions so a Rabbit born under this Sky sign will be an excellent calming influence on anyone. People born under this sign usually do extremely well as counselors. Your lucky day is Saturday.

25. The Sky Horse

This is a lovely Sky sign loved by many people. Also referred to as the mediator of the skies, the Sky Horse takes everyone for a joyride, helping others forget their grievances with great effectiveness. A Rabbit born with this sign tends to be soft spoken and very gentle as a personality. Your lucky day is Sunday.

26. The Sky Deer

This is a generous creature whose spirit of giving endears it to many others. The Sky Deer is often associated with those who make it to a high position and then using their influence and success to benefit many others. A Rabbit born who has this Sky sign is sure to have this dimension of generosity in their personality. Your lucky day is Monday.

27. The Sky Snake

This creature represents imperial authority. The Sky Snake travels on the wings of the Phoenix, always ready to receive applause and the adoration of others. Sky Snakes enjoy the destiny of amazing personal advancement especially in the political arena. A Rabbit who is also a Sky Snake should watch for a good opportunity coming in 2011. Your lucky day is Tuesday.

28. The Sky Worm

Humble as this creature may sound, the Sky Worm aims high and when it succeeds it does so with panache and great style. This is the great surprise of the constellation of lunar mansions because those born under this sign have great perseverance and amazing courage to take risks; success for them comes with a vengeance! The Rabbit with this sign should do well in 2011. Your lucky day is Wednesday.

Determining Your Sky Animal Sign

Example: If your day of birth is
25th October 1975

1. Get the corresponding number for your
   month and **year** from **Table 1** on page 84.
   Thus the number for October is 20, and
   the number for the year 1975 is 14.

2. Next, add the numbers of the month and
   the year to the day in October which is 25.
   Thus 20 + 14 + 25 = 59.

3. Next determine if your year of birth 1937 is
   a leap year; if it is, and you were born after
   March 1st, add 1. Here 1937 is not a leap
   year, and you were born after March 1st, so
   here you do not add 1 to 59.

4. As 59 is more than 56, you need to subtract
   56 from 59. Thus 59 - 56 = 3. So note that
   for you, the Sky Animal is number 3.

To explain this part of the calculation note that since there are 28 animals, any number higher than 28 should deduct 28 and any number higher than 56 which is 28 x 2, should deduct 56 from the total to reach a number that is lower than 28. This will indicate your lunar mansion number.

Once you have your number, which in this example is **3**, Your Sky animal (or lunar mansion) is the one corresponding to the number 3 in Table 2 shown below.

In this example of someone born on 25th October 1975, your Sky animal is the **Sky Beaver** and you belong to the Constellation of the **Green Dragon** of the eastern skies. Your lucky day is **Saturday** and you belong to the constellation season of **Spring**.

Meanwhile based on your year of birth, you are born under the Zodiac sign of the **Wood Rabbit**.

TABLE 1
To Determine the Animal of Your Day of Birth

MONTH	YEAR	YEAR	YEAR	YEAR	YEAR	NO.
-	1920*	1942	-	1987	2009	1
FEB, MAR	-	1943	1965	1988*	2010	2
-	1921	1944*	1966	-	2011	3
-	1922	-	1967	1989	2012*	4
APRIL	1923	1945	1968*	1990		5
-	1924*	1946	-	1991	2013	6
MAY	-	1947	1969	1992*	2014	7
-	1925	1948*	1970	-	2015	8
-	1926	-	1971	1993	2016*	9
JUNE	1927	1949	1972*	1994		10
-	1928*	1950	-	1995	2017	11
JULY	-	1951	1973	1996*	2018	12
-	1929	1952*	1974	-	2019	13
-	1930	-	1975	1997	2020*	14
AUGUST	1931	1953	1976*	1998		15
-	1932*	1954	-	1999	2021	16
-	-	1955	1977	2000*	2022	17
SEPTEMBER	1933	1956*	1978	-	2023	18
-	1934	-	1979	2001	2024*	19
OCTOBER	1935	1957	1980*	2002		20
-	1936*	1958	-	2003	2025	21
-	-	1959	1981	2004*	2026	22
NOVEMBER	1937	1960*	1982	-	2027	23
-	1938	-	1983	2005	2028*	24
DECEMBER	1939	1961	1984*	2006	-	25
-	1940*	1962		2007	2029	26
JANUARY	-	1963	1985	2008*	2030	27
-	1941	1964*	1986	-	2031	28

* indicates a leap year

TABLE 2
The 28 Animals of the Four Constellations

FAMILY OF THE GREEN DRAGON RULING THE SEASON OF SPRING

Lunar Mansion Constellations of the **Eastern** skies

1. **Sky Salamander** THURSDAY
2. **Sky Dragon** FRIDAY
3. **Sky Beaver** SATURDAY
4. **Sky Rabbit** SUNDAY
5. **Sky Fox** MONDAY
6. **Sky Tiger** TUESDAY
7. **Sky Leopard** WEDNESDAY

FAMILY OF THE BLACK TORTOISE RULING THE SEASON OF WINTER

Lunar Mansion Constellations of the **Northern** skies

8. **Sky Unicorn** THURSDAY
9. **Sky Ox** FRIDAY
10. **Sky Bat** SATURDAY
11. **Sky Rat** SUNDAY
12. **Sky Swallow** MONDAY
13. **Sky Boar** TUESDAY
14. **Sky Porcupine** WEDNESDAY

FAMILY OF THE WHITE TIGER RULING THE SEASON OF AUTUMN

Lunar Mansion Constellations of the **Western** skies

15. **Sky Wolf** THURSDAY
16. **Sky Dog** FRIDAY
17. **Sky Pheasant** SATURDAY
18. **Sky Rooster** SUNDAY
19. **Sky Raven** MONDAY
20. **Sky Monkey** TUESDAY
21. **Sky Ape** WEDNESDAY

FAMILY OF THE CRIMSON PHOENIX RULING THE SEASON OF SUMMER

Lunar Mansion Constellations of the **Southern** skies

22. **Sky Ant Eater** THURSDAY
23. **Sky Sheep** FRIDAY
24. **Sky Antler** SATURDAY
25. **Sky Horse** SUNDAY
26. **Sky Deer** MONDAY
27. **Sky Snake** TUESDAY
28. **Sky Worm** WEDNESDAY

Interacting With Others In 2011

Part 4

Harassed Rabbit Needs Friendship & Love More Than Ever

Many factors affect how one animal sign gets along with another and the Chinese believe that much of this has to do with astrological forces that influence personality and attitudes in a particular year. The varying factors result in a difference in compatibility and affinity between different animal signs each year. While it is impossible to take note of everything, the key variables to note are one's chi energy essence and whether the year's constellations are making you feel positive and good about yourself. The influence of the YEAR on the compatibilities of relationships is thus important; you cannot ignore the influence that the annual chi has on the way you interact with your loved ones and family.

New energies influence the way you treat people, in turn determining how they respond to you. Your interactions with close friends and loved ones are affected by your mental and physical state. So how you get on with your partner, your spouse, parents, children, siblings, relatives and friends is affected by your fortunes in any given year. These relationships create important inputs to your happiness.

Understanding compatibilities make you more understanding; so when differences crop up, these need not be taken to heart. Your good vibes make you tolerant but afflictive energies and negative stars suffered by others can make them seem rather tiresome.

Annual energy does influence the people you have greater or lesser affinity with. In some years, you might even feel an inexplicable aversion to someone you may always have liked and loved; or a sudden attraction to someone you previously found annoying! Usually, of course, the affinity groupings, secret friends alliances and ideal soul mate pairings of the Zodiac exert strong influences as well, but annual chi also has the power to sway your thinking and those of others. They can make you more argumentative or make you more loving. People tend to be more or less tolerant or selfish, cold or warm depending on the way things turn out for them from year to year. When life and work goes well, we become better disposed towards others. Then, even a natural zodiac enemy can become a soul mate, if only for a short period of time. Likewise, when one is being challenged by big problems, even the slightest provocation can lead to anger. Zodiac friends and allies might even then appear insufferable. A falling out between Horoscope allies is thus not impossible.

In this section, we examine the Rabbit's personal relationships with the other eleven signs in 2011.

Zodiac Influences
1. Alliance of Allies
2. Zodiac Soulmates
3. Secret Friends
4. Astrology Enemies
5. Peach Blossom
6. Seasonal Trinity

1. Alliance of Allies

Four affinity groupings of animal signs form an alliance of natural allies in the horoscope. The three signs possess similar thought processes, aspirations and goals. Their attitudes are alike, and their support of each other is usually instant and dependable. All three signs having good fortune in any year makes the alliance strong, and if there is an alliance within a family unit as amongst siblings, or between spouses and a child, the family is extremely supportive, giving strength to each other. In good years, auspicious luck gets multiplied. Allies always get along. Any falling out is temporary. They trust each other and close ranks against external threats. Good astrological feng shui comes from carrying the image of your allies, especially when they are going through good years.

ALLY GROUPINGS	ANIMALS	CHARACTERISTICS
COMPETITORS	Rat, Dragon, Monkey	Competent, Tough, Resolute
INTELLECTUALS	Ox, Snake, Rooster	Generous, Focused, Resilient
ENTHUSIASTS	Dog, Tiger, Horse	Aggressive, Rebellious, Coy
DIPLOMATS	Boar, Sheep, Rabbit	Creative, Kind, Emotional

The Rabbit and its allies together make up the numbers 8, 4 and 5 and in 2011 which indicate that of the three it is the Boar is the luckiest. However the Sheep also enjoys the luck of romance in 2011. It is the Rabbit that is afflicted by the wu wang, while the Sheep and Boar each enjoy the auspicious stars of the 24 mountains. So the strongest link in this Alliance is the Boar who enjoys the number 8 star, but Sheep is also good. In 2011 this is not a strong alliance. Boar must carry the year.

Image of the Sheep, Rabbit and Boar as Allies of the Zodiac.

2. Zodiac Soulmates

There are six pairs of animal signs that create six Zodiac Houses of yin and yang soulmates. Each pair creates powerful bonding on a cosmic level. Marriages or business unions between people belonging to the same Zodiac House are extremely auspicious. In a marriage, there is promise of great happiness. In a commercial partnership, it promises much wealth and success. This pairing is also good between professional colleagues and siblings. The strength of each pair is different; with each having a defining strength with some making better commercial than marriage partners. How successful you are as a pair depends on how you bond. The table summarizes the key strength of each Zodiac house.

A coming together of Yin Rabbit with its soul mate the Yang Tiger creates the *House of Growth and Development*; but this is not a strong alliance in 2011. The Rabbit is weak, although the Tiger brings some great energy to the pairing. The Tiger here will take the initiative while the Rabbit tries to keep up and avoid getting in the way. Rabbit and Tiger work well together, so an alliance between them is beneficial, especially for the Rabbit. In this alliance, the Tiger benefits the Rabbit in 2011.

HOUSES OF PAIRED SOULMATES

ANIMALS	YIN/YANG	ZODIAC HOUSE OF CREATIVITY	TARGET UNLEASHED
Rat	YANG	HOUSE OF CREATIVITY & CLEVERNESS	The Rat initiates
Ox	YIN		The Ox completes
Tiger	YANG	HOUSE OF GROWTH & DEVELOPMENT	The Tiger employs force
Rabbit	YIN		The Rabbit uses diplomacy
Dragon	YANG	HOUSE OF MAGIC & SPRITITUALITY	The Dragon creates magic
Snake	YIN		The Snake creates mystery
Horse	YANG	HOUSE OF PASSION & SEXUALITY	The Horse embodies male energy
Sheep	YIN		The Sheep is the female energy
Monkey	YANG	HOUSE OF CAREER & COMMERCE	The Monkey creates strategy
Rooster	YIN		The Rooster get things moving
Dog	YANG	HOUSE OF DOMESTICITY	The Dog works to provide
Boar	YIN		The Boar enjoys what is created

3. Secret Friends

There are six sets of a *secret friendship* that exists between the animal signs of the Zodiac. Between them a very powerful affinity exists making them excellent for each other. Love, respect and goodwill flow freely between secret friends; and they create wonderful happiness vibes for each other in a marriage. Once forged, it is a bond that is hard to break; and even when they themselves want to break, it will be hard for either party to fully walk away. This pair of signs will stick together through thick and thin.

In the pairing of secret friends the Rabbit is paired with the Dog.

PAIRINGS OF SECRET FRIENDS

	Rat	Ox	
	Boar	Tiger	
	Dog	Rabbit	
	Dragon	Rooster	
	Snake	Monkey	
	Horse	Sheep	

4. Astrological Enemies

Then there are the astrological enemies of the Horoscope. This is the sign that directly confronts yours in the Astrology Compass. For the Rabbit, your enemy is the Rooster. Note that the enemy does not necessarily harm you; it only means someone of this sign can never be of any real help to you. But note that the enmity between the Rabbit and the Rooster is reflected in their conflicting elements and their natural hostility.

PAIRINGS OF ASTROLOGICAL ENEMIES

Rat	⟷	Horse
Boar	⟷	Snake
Dog	⟷	Dragon
Rabbit	⟷	Rooster
Tiger	⟷	Monkey
Ox	⟷	Sheep

There is a six year gap between natural enemies. A marriage between them is not usually recommended. Thus marriage between a Rabbit and a Rooster is better avoided unless other indications in their paht chee charts suggest otherwise. Nevertheless pairings between arrows of antagonism are generally discouraged. Rabbit people are advised to refrain from getting involved with a Rooster over the long term, although on a year by year basis, this can sometimes be overcome by the energies of the year. This is definitely not such a year.

As a business partnership, the pairing is likely to be problematic, and in the event of a split, the separation can be acrimonious even if they start out as best friends. In 2011 the Rabbit and the Rooster will find themselves fighting nonstop if they are in business together.

5. Peach Blossom Links

Each of the Alliance of Allies has a special relationship with one of the four primary signs of Horse, Rat, Rooster and Rabbit in that these are the symbolic representations of love and romance for one Alliance group of animal signs.

In the Horoscope, they are referred to as *peach blossom animals*, and the presence of their images in the homes of the matching Alliance of Allies brings peach blossom luck which is associated with love and romance.

The Rabbit belongs to the Alliance of Rabbit, Boar and Sheep, which has the Rat as their peach blossom link. The Rabbit will benefit from associating with anyone born in the Rat year, and will also benefit from placing a painting or image of a Rat in the North corner of the house, or in the Rabbit direction of East.

6. Seasonal Trinity

Another grouping of animal signs creates the four seasonal trinity combinations that bring the luck of seasonal abundance. To many astrology experts, this is regarded as one of the more powerful combinations, and when it exists within a family made up of either parent or both parents and with one or more children, it indicates that collectively, these family members are strong enough to transform all negative luck indications for the family members that make up the combination, for the entire year. The table below summarises the Seasonal groupings.

SEASONAL TRINITIES OF THE HOROSCOPE

ANIMAL SIGNS	SEASON	ELEMENT	DIRECTION
Dragon, Rabbit, Tiger	Spring	Wood	East
Snake, Horse, Sheep	Summer	Fire	South
Monkey, Rooster, Dog	Autumn	Metal	West
Ox, Rat, Boar	Winter	Water	North

Thus when the annual indications of the year are not favourable, the existence of the seasonal combination of animal signs in any living abode can transform the bad luck into better luck especially during the season indicated by the combination. It is necessary for **all** three animal signs to live together in the *same house* or to be in the same office working in close proximity for this powerful pattern to work. For greater impact it is better feng shui if they are all using the direction associated with the relevant seasons. Thus the seasonal combination of Spring is East, while the seasonal combination of Summer is South.

The Rabbit belongs to the combination of Spring, a combination which strengthens its links with the Dragon and the Rabbit. Should a Rabbit and Dragon marry, and they have a Tiger child for instance, the three will create the trinity of spring. With the trinity created, they attract the luck of abundance during the spring season!

Tiger, Rabbit and Dragon, the "*Trinity of Spring*"

RABBIT WITH RAT
In 2011, afflicted by strains & difficulties

The Rabbit who pairs up with a Rat in 2011 will find it hard going. It is a tough relationship for both sides as both signs are afflicted in a serious way. Rabbit is being hit by a very difficult affliction - the five yellow - a star number which brings misfortunes. Rat has the quarrelsome star and will tend to be intolerant. As a result, we see two potentially charming people terribly stressed out and distracted - there is little room to manoeuvre when it comes to working on a love relationship or a business partnership.

The Rabbit usually has no problems getting along with the Rat. As a couple, they fit well into any kind of social environment. But in 2011, there are other factors coming into play. Cosmic chi is simply not on their side. As a result, Rat and Rabbit find their time together not as harmonious as can be. Rat's impatience can cause mild-mannered Rabbit to break out in a temper as well. Indeed, Rabbit, busy coping with its share of cosmic negativities, will find that having to cope with a bad-tempered spouse at the same time is too aggravating to endure. The one consolation is that Rat is blessed with very auspicious constellations and this will help see them through the year. At the end of the day, those who had a good year together last year but who are going through stress of any kind this year will fall back into each other's arms.

If Rat can understand the ferocity of the *wu wang* causing grievous stress to Rabbit, this couple could rumble along through the year and things eventually work themselves out. Both are sensible enough not to allow self-destructive behaviour to destroy what they value, and because they think long term, they eventually allow cool heads to prevail. Both have good instincts, knowing when to make a stand and when to pass. It is this natural antennae of theirs that enables them to stay in sync with each other without saying much.

The 27 year old Wood Rat and 24 year old Fire Rabbit will find it easier than the others, as they are young enough to be excited by their ambitions. Here the older Rat is being favored by the 24 mountains stars and the younger Rabbit will find it comforting leaning on the older Rat. This is a couple still very much in love so there are fewer problems in this relationship. The 39 year old Water Rat and 36 year old Wood Rabbit benefits from their element compatibility. Here, Rat's success indications appear big enough to carry the pair along, with the Rat helping Rabbit ride out the rough year. The good thing is that Rat's Water element strengthens Rabbit's finance luck.

RABBIT WITH OX
Ox leaves Rabbit far behind

The Rabbit in 2011 finds little common ground with the Ox. It is one of the sad things about relationships that things rarely work out when the energy of both sides is different, and in 2011, everything about the Ox and Rabbit is moving in different directions. There is imbalance in this relationship this coming year, as a result of which there is nothing that can bind them to each other; they have absolutely nothing in common.

It is also a hard time for the Rabbit. This is the year when the five yellow afflicts Rabbit and even though it is its year, still, the energy of the year is working against Rabbit and there are obstacles and setbacks to contend with. The Rabbit person is definitely not at its best, not good enough for the high flying Ox.

The Ox in 2011 has a very promising ride with many good things lined up for it, and although its own inner chi essence may not be very strong, the energy of the year brings good winds. There is excitement and the Ox is both optimistic and upbeat, something that grates on the Rabbit. As a result, this pair will tend to annoy one another more than they care to admit. It is an aggravating relationship that does not bring any kind of long-term satisfaction, and it really might be better off for the pair who is dating to move on without one another. In any case, the Rabbit and Ox have little to bind them in a happy long term relationship. Better to part. Ox will always let work come before domesticity, so unlike the Rabbit, has little interest in wanting to make the relationship work.

All of this confirms the natural antipathy that can easily spring up between this pair. They cannot inspire or support each other. Differences in their thought processes and ultimate life goals also draw them apart. The Rabbit is an indulgent person who enjoys the fine things in life, while the Ox is more practical and down to earth, being a no-nonsense and no-frills type of person.

Those already in a marriage or partnership together and who want to maintain their relationship, the best way is for Rabbit to follow its gentle disposition and allow Ox to call the shots. In any case, the year favors the Ox and it is beneficial for both to let the dominating Ox have its way.

RABBIT WITH TIGER
Holding hands with the big cat

Rabbit and Tiger rarely ignore one another on first meeting. They have something special that breathes life into their relationship. There is an instant warming to each other and affinity develops quickly. It is just like last year except in 2011, the Tiger is drawn to a Rabbit in distress. This year sees Rabbit suffering from the mortal blows of feng shui afflictions. This might put off those who sense the smell of Rabbit's discomfort and shy away, but not the Tiger. The big cat responds positively and becomes a shoulder and a good friend, somehow pumping new energy by sheer force of friendship and loving. The Rabbit will respond with warmth and candor. It takes them no time at all to develop something serious between them irrespective of who is taking the initiative and who is responding.

Like last year, both Rabbit and Tiger make appearances in the 2011 paht chee chart and this enhances their contemporary energy chi. Tiger appears twice in the chart just like last year, and is next to the Rabbit - again just like last year. This indicates excellent signals of auspiciousness for these two people coming together. They develop a closeness quickly; their attitudes and opinions resonate easily off each other as they bounce ideas and exchange confidences. It is all very natural. It does not matter about the gender, the attraction between these two signs is obvious and even electric! They will mirror each other's tastes and attitudes, finding common ground at different levels spiritually and intellectually. Their horoscope and astrological perspectives cause them to work and play to the same rhythm. This has its source in their strong connection to the Season of Spring, which highlights the renewal and birth of things, and because they are intrinsically Wood element people, they are mindful of the vital ingredients needed in the growth process.

If they work or do business together, it is easy to blend their skills together, conducive to achieving the most productive results. Their methods may not be the same, but as a team, they are effective. Like last year, in 2011 they benefit from Dragon energy, so attracting a Dragon partner, having a Dragon child or just enhancing their space with a Dragon image benefits them.

Two sets of pairings - the 49 year old Water Tiger and 48 year old Water Rabbit as well as the 25 year old Fire Tiger/24 year old Fire Rabbit - continue on a roll through 2011 as they continue to experience prosperity and growth despite new obstacles. Together they will successfully create the *House of Growth and Development* for their families.

RABBIT WITH RABBIT
Two of a kind huddling close

Those who belong to the sign of the Rabbit are
naturally close buddies who look out for one another.
They do this like it is second nature, so in a year of trials
and tribulations like 2011 looks to be, they will grow
even closer, exuding synergistic strength and a unified
front that is quite impressive to observe. This sign has
patience and is also resilient - in the face of adversity
with things going wrong and having to confront bad
luck in its unexpected manifestations, the Rabbit can
usually stay quite calm. Their first instincts are always
to run, take flight, hide... this is the Rabbit's instinctive
response to danger, so with two of them, this tendency
strengthens. This is something that is plain to see in
2011 when things tend to get a bit rough.

The Rabbit has to endure some rather adverse obstacles
brought by feng shui afflictions. The nasty *wu wang* or
five yellow brings cause for concerns - illness, setbacks
and even misunderstandings with friends and allies - it
seems that few things go smooth and even less go right,
especially since the Rabbit also faces the affliction of
the three killings from the opposite direction, that of its
natural and astrological foe, the Rooster.

Should you wish to commit to each other, 2011 is as good a year as any to do so, and also to renew your love for each other. Any marriage between Rabbits will see their affinity grow stronger than ever. Plus Rabbits are very much into sharing everything they have, the good with the bad. Family and friends take prime importance in their lives and are high on their priority. If you are a Rabbit, it is lovely being attached to another Rabbit because you do bring out the good in one another, being neither aggressive nor temperamental. Rabbits dislike arguments and always prefer taking the soft to the hard approach.

Rabbits make better colleagues than bosses because they do tend to prevaricate and can be indecisive. Other signs do not really understand or appreciate them like their own kind do. As a result, they tend to be closer to their family members than to outsiders. For them, blood is always thicker than water.

In 2011, Rabbit's life force is not as strong as their spiritual essence. So they will endure and prevail because of their inner strength. The 48 year old Water Rabbit enjoys excellent financial luck. The 24 year old Fire Rabbit likewise enjoys good fortune too, so for these two Rabbits, your love life moves along more smoothly than for other Rabbits. But obstacles do crop up.

RABBIT WITH DRAGON
Tea & sympathy from the Dragon

The Rabbit has good affinity with the sign of the Dragon. It is their seasonal affinity which draws them to each other, because as personalities, they cannot be more different. Their compatibility lies more in opposites attracting than to any similarity in their thought processes or their aspirations. But they do like the same kinds of people and are drawn to the same kind of movie shows or TV programs. And both are equally house proud, so this is a couple who can live together quite harmoniously.

In 2011, the Dragon is drawn to the Rabbit's obvious need for a friend as it negotiates a year filled with problems and continuing troubles. Rabbit's distress makes Dragon conscious of its own strength, even though in truth, the Dragon's life force is not exactly brimming with energy.

What is good about this relationship is the relative absence of competitive pressures between them. The Rabbit will make sure there is little, if any, ego bashing between them, and in a Rabbit Year, the Dragon is also happy to just be around. The good thing is that the mere presence of the Dragon is beneficial for the Rabbit. This is an elemental thing and arises from the connection with the season of Spring. The three signs – Tiger, Rabbit and Dragon – create the seasonal combination of Spring, and all three benefit from Water. There is already the presence of two Tigers in the year's paht chee chart, so all that is needed is the element of Water to benefit this pair.

Water will magnify their luck for the year and make things even better between them. Just by being together, the Rabbit and Dragon create auspicious luck for themselves, so the Dragon will be helping the Rabbit overcome its bad star afflictions without having to do anything except be around.

> The 2011 luck of the Dragon is better than that of the Rabbit, enjoying excellent heavenly luck as well as benefiting from the star of *Small Auspicious*. So in this year, it is the Dragon who must be the stronger of the two and take care of the Rabbit!

The 24 year old Fire Rabbit and 48 year old Water Rabbit enjoy better luck than the other Rabbits, and Dragons attached to them are sure to benefit. Nevertheless, all Rabbits require tea and sympathy, and if your love is a Dragon sign person, you will be more than satisfied.

RABBIT WITH SNAKE
A cool relationship that goes nowhere

In 2011 this relationship seems cool to one another
and any coming together seems doomed to dissolve
in the chilly atmosphere generated by the Snake.
This couple had some happier times last year but in
2011, the Snake cools off and starts to distance itself,
slithering away with little fanfare.

Much of the lack of compatibility comes from their
extremely disparate energies in 2011. The Snake is
strong, vibrant, confident and in search of adventure
with new worlds to conquer. The Rabbit is just the
opposite, suffering from apathy and coping with trials
and tribulations that force it to focus on maintenance
rather than new growth. There is just no meeting
of minds here, not unless Rabbit is prepared for
heartbreak and disappointment. Better to hop away
and split as this is a relationship that benefits neither
of you, at least not this year.

The Rabbit and Snake have never been very
compatible. It is quite difficult expecting them to
ignite any great passion together, and in 2011, it is
even unlikely that the Snake could respond in any way
positive to the Rabbit. Snake may be riding high this
year, but it is reserving its charm for someone equally

ambitious and interested in the same things. Rabbit is still going through a low energy year, while Snake is high voltage, a star in every sense. There is simply no meeting of minds here, unless Rabbit finds Snake an exciting challenge and exerts all its charm to woo the Snake. If this is the situation, then the Rabbit should take note that the Snake finds sexy people irresistible. The Snake also responds to flattery and seduction; to confident people, it is important to come across a winner and to be intellectually stimulating.

But the Rabbit should also appreciate that in a romantic entanglement with the Snake, should they become a couple, it is a relationship that will always have its ups and downs, and maybe more downs. The Rabbit must accept that the Snake can freeze out of the relationship with little warning. Sad but true!

The Rabbit simply cannot take things easy in the company of the Snake; and what is worse is that you, the Rabbit, feel awed by the cool Snake. This can easily deteriorate into annoyance with Rabbit becoming disillusioned. So on balance, it is advisable not to let this relationship go too far. If you are already married, it is a good idea to find common ground so that shared interests become the unifying force that cements your relationship.

RABBIT WITH HORSE
Goodwill turns quickly to ill feeling

In 2011, the Horse and Rabbit make an unlikely pair. The Horse will simply move too fast even for the agile and fast-paced Rabbit. They will also be running in opposite directions, so if they are not already a couple, it is likely that any goodwill at the start soon turns boring and generates ill feelings.

True, the Horse does not exactly have super energy, but the Horse will not be attracted to the Rabbit's aura this year. And even between a married pair comprising Horse and Rabbit, there is a switching off. The Rabbit's aura is afflicted by the negative energy of the *wu wang* or five yellow, making it unattractive, especially to the Horse. It is just hard for the Rabbit to conjure up high energy ambience.

In any case, the Rabbit is not a sign that jumps willy nilly into a romantic relationship, even though the Horse is not averse to a romp every now and again. But in 2011, there is little attraction between them. There are no zodiac or astrological ties binding them, so they are unlikely to warm to each other. They are also not the kind to become bosom pals.

The Horse can be something of a wild child, glad to try anything, and Rabbit is just nothing of this kind, so to you, the Horse is too undisciplined and too different to endear itself to you. The Horse is a free-spirit constantly in search of adventure, while Rabbit is not interested in searching out new places or in climbing the mountains of Nepal. Besides, the Rabbit is too distracted coping with a difficult year when many things go wrong and when it has to spend a good deal of time putting out fires. So the Rabbit has no time to look after a wild child.

If you are a couple, married to each other or living together, the year 2011 is sure to be a trying time for you both. Misunderstandings and arguments crop up regularly. It is just so vital that you, the Rabbit do not have any high expectations from your partner or spouse. They cannot understand you or your insistence on making sure the family and home are kept safe and untroubled. They will not even appreciate your efforts to correct things that go wrong. So the more you realize and accept this, the better the year will turn out to be for you.

You have the discipline and resilience to stand on your own; what's more, if you allow the Horse to have its way and go run in the wild, you would both have an easier time going through the year.

RABBIT WITH SHEEP
Allies in need of yang chi create their own

In 2011, the Rabbit turns to its ally the Sheep for support and a strong shoulder, and the Sheep does not disappoint. Here, the astrological affinity between these two signs ignites goodwill and encouragement, and Sheep, whose energy is both loving and giving in 2011 will shore up its friend and ally, the Rabbit.

The Rabbit has a troubled year filled with countless things going awry, while the Sheep is enjoying brand new *Earth Seal* energy which is both invigorating and inspiring. The Sheep is also very creative, being bitten by the intellectual and entrepreneurial bug. And since the Sheep can be big-hearted by nature, there is more than enough room in its mandala to offer space to its astrological ally.

As a result, the Rabbit responds with grace and vivacity, rolling up its sleeves and falling with the energy of the Sheep. Together they create a new brand of yang chi which opens new vistas and doorways for both. This is a mutually satisfying relationship in 2011, for one brings out the good in the other.

They will get high indulging in the same things, so a natural compatibility starts to unfold for them; an awareness of the artistic and creative flair they generate

together. This brings them happiness and for the Rabbit, it is both comforting and nurturing. In essence, this is what love is all about. The more Sheep lends the Rabbit an ear and a shoulder for support, the more they become soul mates, so 2011 becomes then a good binding year. Trust develops between the pair and this itself is usually strong enough for them both to transform negative energies into good.

> They become comfortable looking out for each other; and then a quiet rapport and sense of comradeship develops. In 2011, the Sheep's restful energy and the Rabbit's resilience continues to generate sweet resonance, so that despite it being a rather tough year for Rabbit, as a pair, they overcome bad vibes to create their own yang-drenched sanctuary.

Any problems that may surface between them will be due to the Rabbit's afflictive state in 2011, being hit by the *wu wang* or five yellow. This is the star of misfortune and it is usually associated with a variety of ills including problems in relationships, ill health and a vulnerability to misunderstandings and quarrels. The *wu wang* brings all sorts of unexpected problems to the Rabbit, but this is overcome, especially when Rabbit pairs up with Sheep.

RABBIT WITH MONKEY
Antagonism brings unhappiness

The Rabbit and Monkey are just so aggravating for each other! These are two signs that simply cannot get along, and if you are already hitched, this new year does not bring any kind of respite, as one just finds the other hard to tolerate and impossible to live with. This pairing is a case of mutual antagonism creating unhappiness, intolerance and dissatisfaction.

In terms of this natural antagonism, 2011 is not any different from last year, except that the Rabbit is going through a year of feng shui afflictions so that for Rabbit, 2011 will be even harder to bear. The indications for the year for the Monkey are a lot better, so here we will see the Monkey being the impatient one, intolerant of Rabbit's difficulties and setbacks. It becomes then quite an impossible situation for them if they are living together, forced to endure each other's hostile energy. All through the year, there could be a simmering resentment.

For those who have just met, any initial attraction soon dissolves away, withers so fast neither quite knows what happens. But it is just as well, because if there is a coming together, it is unlikely to be the kind of loving which inspires the Rabbit or makes your heart soar.

The Rabbit will tire of Monkey's spoilt brat exploits sooner rather than later, and because Monkey's inner essence is marginally stronger than that of the Rabbit's, the Monkey's will could call the day and Rabbit could allow itself to get seduced by the Monkey's charm.

But they cannot last. There is little loving between them. And what there is, is neither deeply moving nor emotionally satisfying.

The Rabbit, though resilient and patient, must cope with the *wu wang* or 5 yellow affliction which brings setbacks, disappointments and hindrances. So Rabbit tends to be less good tempered. so Rabbit ends up being very annoying and coming across unreasonable to Monkey - setting the stage for them to split.

From Rabbit's viewpoint then, it really is better not to have any kind of expectations from a love affair started with a Monkey; in fact, do not take your eyes off other potentials, because you will eventually discover that it really is better looking elsewhere for love. Should you be involved with a Monkey, you will need a reservoir of good intentions and tons of patience. The Monkey is not known for its fidelity so unless you are in it with your eyes wide open, better to split.

RABBIT WITH ROOSTER
Aversion as ill feelings arise

Oh my, what a bad year for these two! Challenging indeed for both Rabbit and Rooster who find that it is already hard enough to look after oneself without also having to cope with a natural enemy's bad vibes at the same time! The Rabbit and Rooster are astrological foes of the Zodiac who under any circumstances have little loyalty towards one another. In 2011 whatever goodwill there may be is put on the back burner. The year of the Rabbit bring trials and tribulations to these two signs so any coming together in an intimate relationship is literally a recipe for disaster.

Both go through a year when the feng shui chart is extremely unkind to them and indeed, based on the Chinese Almanac, the Rooster appear to be having a potentially disastrous year, with direct conflict with the *Tai Sui*, playing host to the *three killings*, as well as the *Natural Disaster* star AND not to mention also directly facing the *wu wang* opposite. It could all be just a bit much for even the mighty strong Rooster to cope. These afflictions are certain to make the Rooster quite impossible to live with. Enter Rabbit who is not having a rosy year either. The Rabbit has its own fair share of tribulations in 2011, so all this negative energy is bound to adversely affect the emotional well being of both signs - causing stress and strain to pull them apart.

That they already have so little goodwill for one another makes things worse. It is advisable for this couple not to start anything. If they are already married, it is vital they support one another in 2011, otherwise both suffer. Should there be a battle between these two, however, it will be the Rooster who will prevail, because Rooster enjoys the power of 9, and Rooster's life force in 2011 is a lot stronger.

Rabbit should understand this and avoid any direct clash with Rooster. Better to walk quietly away than to engage in a noisy fight. If you are in a contentious situation with the Rooster, Rabbit must accept that any relationship with Rooster simply cannot sustain over the long term. It is unrealistic to expect a pairing of zodiac foes to stay good forever! The Chinese Zodiac warns that the Rabbit/ Rooster pair is sure to eventually turn hostile; and the hostility can be ugly.

Rabbit's rising Sun is at odds with Rooster's setting sun. Rabbit symbolizes Spring when growth is vibrant. Rooster personifies Fall, getting ready for Winter. The Wood of Rabbit must fear the Metal of Rooster. Rabbit is better off avoiding the Rooster!

RABBIT WITH DOG
Leaning on Dog's kindness

The Rabbit who is in love with a Dog sign is lucky indeed, because here you have someone who is not just going through a relatively strong year and is thus able to support and nurture you, but this is also a person capable of great kindness. The Dog is famous for being a good friend to anyone close to them, and as you the Rabbit are a secret friend of the Dog, you are likely to benefit more than any others in your relationship with the Dog.

But the Rabbit already instinctively knows this, as you are more than likely to gravitate to people born under the Dog sign without much prompting. In a year when you need real and true friends, you will not trust anyone too readily; the lovely aura of the Dog's energy however will be like a magnet for you.

The Dog enjoys a year when its energy is radiant and glowing. This is a sign who will also have some ups and downs in its luck quota for the year, but all this pales into insignificance as the Dog enjoys the mighty power of 8. This is such a strong indication that in many ways, this could even turn out to be a spectacular year for the Dog.

The Rabbit on the other hand must endure the *wu wang* or five yellow, so in terms of chi energy, there is something of a mismatch here. But because there are binding ties caused by the horoscope, far from being turned off, the Rabbit and Dog find being needed both satisfying and fulfilling.

If this pair are already married, the Dog's energy should carry them through the year, helping Rabbit to survive its afflictions. Between this couple there is genuine trust and understanding. They aspire to the same meaningful things in life and are in tune with each other's moods, attitudes and preferences. This is potentially a very happy marriage as they can be good friends as well as good lovers.

The setback here for this pair is that in 2011, both Rabbit and Dog are rather lacking in energy; they must work at galvanising each other, giving strength and building one another's confidence. The good thing about the Rabbit and Dog is that irrespective of their luck, this does not affect the quality of their relationship and they are as loving during good or bad times. Their genuine affection for each other is usually strong enough to ride through any obstacles and setbacks that may arise.

RABBIT WITH BOAR
Getting big help from lucky Boar

In 2011 Rabbit finds comfort in the company of the happy, very relaxed and very lucky Boar. Indeed, this is a year when the Boar brings exceptional good support to the Rabbit, as its Water element feeds a thirsty Wood Rabbit! This is such a significant aspect of their relationship and it accounts for the natural affinity and compatibility between this pair.

> These are two signs of the Zodiac whose energies are very much in sync. They are allies of course, but more than that, their elements are just so good for each other.

The Rabbit benefits more from this relationship, but the Boar feels good being able to bring benefits to the relationship. The personality of the Boar is both endearing and easy to get along with. There is a quiet humor in the way the Boar carries itself, and as a result, the Rabbit cannot help but be moved and touched.

The Rabbit is not at its best in 2011, unlike the Boar who enjoys the auspicious power of 8 and is also flanked by the stars of *Big* and *Small Auspicious*. Plus the Boar also has the much needed Water element and this makes the year 2011 very beneficial indeed. Everyone belonging to the Rabbit sign benefits from a relationship with the Boar for this reason as well, irrespective of its heavenly stem. This is how the Rabbit will be supported through the year despite its afflictions. If you are already married to a Boar, count your blessings.

If you are just starting out in a love relationship with someone in the sign of the Boar, also count your blessings. You cannot have found a better match. For you, the year will flow more easily and you will find that life takes on new meaning as well. There is nothing that can beat the wonderful effect of finding one's soul mate and this is exactly what this relationship is like.

It is thus worthwhile investing time and effort nurturing this relationship. It is beneficial both long and short term, so make the investment!

Rabbit's Monthly Horoscope 2011

Part 5

Avoiding Bad Vibes & Staying Resilient

This won't be an easy year for the Rabbit, but if you are forewarned and take the necessary remedial measures, you can overcome the setbacks that come your way. The five yellow which makes its way into your home location has the potential to cause bothersome trials and tribulations, but it won't be anything you cannot handle. Your intrinsic element of Wood in itself serves to counter the afflicted Earth energy to an extent. Nevertheless, this is a year when you should avoid taking risks. Lie low and do things in moderation. And don't attract the attention of others by being boastful or showy, as this will only breed envy and resentment.

1ST MONTH
February 4th - March 5th 2011

YEAR STARTS WELL WITH POWER OF HEAVEN

The start of the year brings luck from the heavens, where you get your fair share of opportunities which show themselves in varied and sometimes unexpected ways. Business and career luck is good, and this is a time when you can clinch whatever deal or result you are after. You are not short of allies and are blessed with people luck. Even if difficulties arise, there will always be some guardian angel with arm outstretched to bail you out or give you a helping hand. It is recommended that you boost this kind of luck by carrying or displaying your horoscope allies (Boar and Sheep) and secret friend (Dog), especially when the annual star in your sector is afflicted.

WORK & CAREER - *Good Things in Store*

This is a month when good things come to those of you who are patient. You have hidden supporters when it comes to your career. Accept help and advice graciously. You yourself are not that strong this year in terms of personal energy, but you enjoy a likeability that endears you to many. If you have the right kind of supporters backing you, you have the potential to go far this month. For those of you actively climbing the career ladder, or those of you looking for new jobs, this month could open up exciting possibilities for you. Be clear about what you want, but at the same time, be a little open-minded. New opportunities that seem alien and unthinkable at first could become more exciting on second examination, so don't turn down any offers point blank.

BUSINESS - *Big Break*

Your big break may come this month, brought to you by friends or acquaintances you already know, or even by a total stranger. When others want to make friends with you, oblige. Enlarging your circle of friendship and alliances now will only help you through the course of a challenging year. Do not push aside any opportunity without considering carefully first. There could be something awesomely exciting in store for you, if only you're astute enough to spot it.

To actualize your aspirations, you can use the help of a **wishfulfilling jewel**; use a yellow one for aspirations involving wealth or material gains, a red one for reputation, and a green one for growth. Make a wish while focusing on your crystal. Use one crystal per wish. Even better is to get a wishfulfilling jewel with mantras.

LOVE & RELATIONSHIPS - *Follow Your Heart*

A romantic month lies ahead for the Rabbit. You feel more compassionate and kindly, and others are drawn by this aspect of your personality. When you turn on the charm, you are definitely hard to resist. Single Rabbits have a lot of success in the dating game, while married ones can expect their partners to sit up and take more notice of them this month.

Go with the flow if you are faced with tough decisions related to love. Follow your heart, for it will tell you the right thing this month. You are blessed with divine energy this month, so nothing can go far wrong. And for those of you who really want to enjoy, as long as there's a will there is definitely a way.

EDUCATION - *Luck Shines Bright*

Things go easy for the young Rabbit this month. There are many reasons for you to feel encouraged and to build self-confidence. When your luck shines brightly, there is nothing better than to try just that little bit harder. Effort translates into results easily during months like this, so make the most of it.

2ND MONTH
March 6th - April 4th 2011

MISFORTUNES MOUNT & PROBLEMS APPEAR

This is a highly dangerous month for the Rabbit, as the monthly five yellow has flown in to join the annual five yellow in your home location. This is like a double whammy of bad luck, but the good news is that there is also completion luck that comes with it. Even if unfortunate things happen to you, once they are over it is like having used up a whole load of bad karma. But while one can put a positive spin on anything, it still pays to be more alert and more careful this month. Don't put yourself in a situation of danger, and wear a **mantra ring** or necklace to keep you safe against harm. Lady Rabbits can also carry the **Nightspot amulet** or hang from your handbag.

Wear a **mantra ring** or or mantra collier to bring protection against danger and harm this month.

WORK & CAREER - *Keep your Wits*

Watch out for troublemakers at work. People may not be out to get you, as you might sometimes feel, but you could become a casualty of war in someone else's burning ambition to rise to the top. Don't let yourself be made use of. Keep your wits about you. If you work in a competitive environment, watch others don't make you look bad simply so they look good in comparison. This is a fast-paced month when slip-ups get spotted quickly, and it is easy to make mistakes. Don't work yourself to the ground by trying too hard. A fresh mind beats a tired one anytime, and you'll need to be sharp and on the ball, so don't get fooled into thinking productivity is proportionate to hours put in.

BUSINESS - *Avoid Taking Risks*

Not a great month for Rabbits in business. Unexpected circumstances could crop up making your life very difficult. Your negative luck could ripen in different ways. Don't put yourself in any financially risky situation. Avoid investing big, entering into new partnerships, pursuing new ventures or entering unchartered territory this month. Wait till your fortunes improve before becoming overly brave. Good ideas are best put on the backburner for implementation later. Otherwise you could just get burnt.

LOVE & RELATIONSHIPS - *Fragile*

This is no month to pursue your love life with any degree of seriousness, because love luck unfortunately looks rather poorly. Don't wear your heart on your sleeve unless you have skin as thick as a buffalo's hide. Not that you would get hurt for sure, but the chances are you're more emotionally fragile now than ever, and the smallest thing could set you off, and spiral out of control. You have enough to worry about with other areas of your life, you don't need romance issues to add to a pile of problems. Married Rabbits should cut their spouses some slack. Your moodiness could grate on the nerves of your other half. If you want a harmonious marriage, you should put in some effort also.

EDUCATION - *Character-Building*

If things seem difficult when it comes to schoolwork, don't worry yourself too much over it. Wear a **pagoda** amulet or carry a **Good Education** amulet to help you concentrate in class. If you need help, don't hesitate to ask or make your teachers dedicate some extra time for you. Things get way better next month for the student Rabbit, so treat any stumbling blocks along the way as character building opportunities.

Carry the **Education Amulet** to improve study luck especially if you are sitting important exams.

3RD MONTH
April 5th - May 5th 2011

FINDING RESPITE WIITH LOVED ONES

This promises to be a much better month than last for the Rabbit. While things may have been difficult in the recent past, this month you get valuable support from friends and supporters, while loved ones provide much appreciated moral support and encouragement. Work relationships improve and you find yourself getting along much better with your co-workers. The backbiting environment of last month evaporates, and now most people seem to be on your side. Avoid anyone who makes you feel bad about yourself. There is good fortune in your chart, so make the most of it by fraternizing only with those who will bring out the best in you. You can afford to be a bit choosy about your friends right now.

WORK & CAREER - *Spotlight on You*

Work smart this month and you could catch the eye of someone influential who can do much for your future in your career. Luck on the work front is excellent this month so make the most of it. Giving this aspect of your life more attention now will pay off handsomely. Put forward good ideas and don't be afraid to take a more dominant role in discussions. You're persuasive and others will be impressed with your input. Some tempting offers could come your way this month, but don't make your mind up on anything major without thinking things through carefully.

BUSINESS - *Networking Luck*

This is a productive time to dedicate to meeting more people and making contacts. Intelligent networking could lead to something exciting. Put your skill with people and your natural flair for making friends to good use this month. New partnerships struck up now hold out much promise for the future. An especially auspicious time to launch a new product or service, and to invest in new marketing efforts. An unexpected individual could turn out to be of bigger help than you at first realize.

LOVE & RELATIONSHIPS - *Passion Abounds*

A great time lies ahead for the Rabbit looking for love. There's a high chance of success for any relationships that get struck up this month, especially of the romantic kind! Passion is pulsing under your skin and you're happiest when you have the attention of someone special. You are not short on admirers, but don't be overly picky with who you will date and who is out of the question; a beautiful relationship that's most unexpected could be struck up this month. Let your heart lead your head to a certain extent, and don't be overly guarded. The Rabbit who dares to let go and dream will reap the biggest rewards this month.

For the married Rabbit, this is an ideal time to renew the passion in your marriage. There's a certain magic in putting in real effort to rekindling the flames of love. Make time to indulge in the frivolous and light-hearted. Those of you looking for feng shui help to rekindle a love spark, display a beautiful **Rat figurine** in the North of your bedroom. This activates powerful peach blossom luck for you.

EDUCATION - *Superb Study Luck*

Study luck shines on you this month. Learning new things becomes easy and previously dull subjects come alive for you. Make the best of this lucky time by making an effort to pay attention in class. Use your scholastic luck this month to jump onto a higher plane of learning. You can leapfrog several levels this month, so start setting higher standards for yourself. Don't try to do everything yourself though; if you need any help, ask for it. This will speed up the learning process.

4TH MONTH
May 6th - June 5th 2011

HOSTILITY & ANTAGONISM ALL ROUND

Unfortunately this is a rather quarrelsome month for the Rabbit person. You will find yourself losing your temper more than usual as there is plenty of argumentative chi in the air. Petty bickering can become serious very quickly, so don't let arguments and misunderstandings get out of hand. Avoid picking fights with people and beware of offending the wrong person. You could end up with a lawsuit in your hands. Whenever you find your temper flaring up, take a deep breath and resist the urge to explode. Your anger will soon pass and each time you will thank yourself for being in control of your emotions.

WORK & CAREER - *Challenging*

This could be a rather challenging month. Together with being more bad tempered than usual, working long hours and working to deadlines are likely to get you down. You could feel that what is expected of you is unfair; when you stop expecting everything to be non-discriminatory is when you'll start to enjoy your work more and perform better in your career. Use the unjustness of it all to your advantage. Turn things to your favor with your charm, then back up that charm by delivering results. If others seem to be picking on you, instead of feeling sorry for yourself, win them over on to your side. Place a **Ru Yi** on your desk to help you make good decisions at work, and to put yourself in a position of power vis a vis your co-workers.

BUSINESS - *Keep A Watch On Your Finances*

Watch out for disgruntled characters that bear a grudge against you. They may be out to get you this month. It is important for Rabbits in business to enhance personal luck as much as possible to keep misfortune at bay. Avoid activating the East sector with anything noisy. Any windchimes placed here need to be removed this month. Keep activity to a minimum in the East. Noise in this area will intensify animosity this month. Business luck does not look promising this month, with an indication of money troubles to come. Keep a watch on your finances. Cash flow may not be so healthy but as long as you are forewarned and guard against overexposure, you should ride through OK. Use the **Lock Coin** to protect your wealth; sleep with one under your pillow and keep one in your drawer or in your invoice book at work.

LOVE - *Not Easy*

This is not an easy month for Rabbits when it comes to love. There is too much quarrelsome chi in your chart for anyone to get close enough to start something serious with you. Those of you wanting to take your relationship further will have to put in a superhuman effort not to be so easily riled. The more secure your current relationship, the more you have to worry. Familiarity can breed contempt this month, so keep this in mind when interacting with a love mate. Married Rabbits especially should be careful their tempers do not drive their spouses into the arms of others. Wear a **Peace amulet** to control the argument chi in your chart this month and should you fight, back down, because there is nothing to gain (and everything to lose) from winning.

Wear or carry a **Ping peace amulet** to improve love relationships this month.

5TH MONTH
June 6th - July 6th 2011

REDUCING ENERGY BRINGS ILLNESS

This is not a month to take risks as the illness and accident start pays a visit. Try not to plan big life events for this month. The chi energy in your chart is extremely afflicted by malevolent Earth stars, so it is a good idea to try and wear more precious Metal energy to counter this. Wearing gold is considered best, especially when fashioned into auspicious symbols of good fortune. For those of you prone to getting sick, wear a **golden Wu Lou** on a chain. Avoid physically risky activities and rough sports. And remember, this is no time to be taking any risks. If you feel uneasy about something, trust your instincts this month.

WORK & CAREER - *Friendships Matter*

Watch out for troublemakers at the workplace. While Rabbits pursuing demanding careers could find the month stressful, at least you will have a clear picture of who's on your side and who isn't. You have friendship and ally luck, even if everything else is looking rather dismal, and this is the time when you may have to count on your friendships with your co-workers.

Beware of floating aimlessly in the workplace. You could recurrently find yourself at a loose end with all tasks complete. Make yourself more useful and expend your job scope if things are looking a little light for you. If you become redundant, you could well be made redundant, so don't go down that road. Seize the initiative to be as useful as possible when it comes to your work and career.

BUSINESS - *Much To Learn*

This month you could find yourself having more contact and interaction with other key players in the industry. You have plenty to learn from your competitors and those in similar businesses as you. You may enter into a competitive situation with some of them, but may well synergize and join forces with some others. Good possibilities of teaming up may crop up this month. While it is worthwhile to pursue, try not to finalize anything till next month, when your luck is better.

LOVE & RELATIONSHIPS - *Play It Cool*

Beware of wearing your heart on your sleeve. You could well get it broken. Don't open your heart too quickly to just anyone. If your love interest is not showing you the same kind of commitment as you're prepared to put into the relationship, see it as a warning sign. Don't appear overly keen because this will put off the other party. This month it is better to play it a little cool. In fact, if you have other things in life to focus on, best to leave love alone for now. Not a good month to get married or to go steady. For those of you who are married, wear a golden **double happiness symbol**. Or you can wear a golden **rooster with fan and amethyst** if your marriage is at risk of being plundered by a third party. While there is risk of a roving eye from your partner, you yourself could also be vulnerable to the charms of an outside third party.

Wear the **double happiness symbol** for a strong and secure marriage or relationship.

EDUCATION - *Tougher*

School and studies may be tougher this month because of a lack of time. Other demands in your life in the form of a social life, sport or hobby may distract you from your studies. You may be having a great time outside the classroom, but you could also be doing so much better when it comes to schoolwork. Don't let your grades slip when they don't need to.

6TH MONTH
July 7th - Aug 7th 2011

RISING ABOVE DIFFICULTIES AS YOU GET STRONGER

Things improve from last month for you. You will find things proceed more smoothly and there will be fewer obstacles in your path. Projects get completed more easily and your relationships with others improve. This is a month of new beginnings when you may experiences some changes that bring exciting new things into your life. Things started now enjoy a good chance of success, so this is not the time to rest on your laurels. Put extra effort into everything you do as it will be more than worth it!

WORK & CAREER - *Options*

This is a busy time for the Rabbit at work. When you've completed one task, another gets set. It is a long road this month, but being this busy keeps you satisfied. You enjoy your job, especially if your boss appreciates you. Those of you thinking about changing jobs or career can afford to seriously think about it now. You have the luck to embark on new things. But before you make serious decisions that have the potential to affect your future significantly, think things through carefully. You don't want to make an impulse decision that you will regret later on. This is a good time however to showcase your talents as recognition luck is good, so don't jump ship the minute something you think is better comes along. It may just be worth it to stick it out at what you're already doing and build on from there.

BUSINESS - *Can Go All Out*

Money luck is good this month, so those of you who are your own boss should go all out to expand sales and income. This is a good time to pitch for new jobs, attract new clients and embark on a new marketing drive. Expansion is fruitful and will be met with success. You can afford to invest and think how else you'd like to achieve more.

Prosperity luck is strong. Enhance this by installing a new **wealth ship** in the office, or by making a new **wealth vase** to add to your collection. You are in an optimistic frame of mind and others look up to you as a relevant leader. Your management skills are enhanced this month, and it is a good time to galvanize and motivate the staff. Spend effort nurturing your employees and the people who work with you. A little time and effort will go a long way this month.

LOVE & RELATIONSHIPS - *Distracted*

This month you may be a little distracted when it comes to love. Rabbits in steady relationships may have to make a conscious effort to give enough attention to their other halves. You tend to be more preoccupied with work and business than with your love life, and at times this month, this is to the serious detriment of your relationship. Try and bring some balance into your life. Rabbits whose partners work alongside them will probably become closer to their partners, while if you're from totally different worlds workwise, you may start to drift apart. Recognize if this is happening and make an effort to spend some quality time together. Watch for outside third parties elbowing their way into your relationship. While you are preoccupied elsewhere, your better half could be being wooed by an outsider out to cause trouble.

EDUCATION - *Can Shine*

The Rabbit in school does well in leadership roles this month. Your personal chi is strong and you do very well in both academic and other pursuits. Let your intellect shine by putting more effort in your work. Make an effort to contribute in class and initiate discussions with your teachers. The more you pursue knowledge this month, the more you will benefit from the positive Chi that surrounds you this month.

7TH MONTH
Aug 8th - Sept 7th 2011

FORGING AHEAD WITH RESILIENCE & RESOLVE

You can make big strides in your pursuits this month, but this is not as auspicious a time as last month for the Rabbit-born. There is a chance that small mishaps can become bigger problems if you don't put a stop to them early on. However, don't let yourself get stressed out over small things. You may run into some bad luck in the form of cash flow problems or unexpected expenditures, so this is not the best time to splash out if you're tight financially. In your dealings with others, avoid arguments and steer yourself away from people who rile you up. Expend energy in things that matter. Don't let obstacles that crop up worry you too much. Take them in your stride. Those of you with strong resilience and resolve will get through the month much more successfully than those of you who sweat the small stuff.

WORK & CAREER - *Potholes to Maneuver*

This is a fast-paced month with potholes to maneuver. Stay alert at the workplace. Don't let your guard down.

There may be opportunities for some to shine at the expense of others, especially for those of you working in competitive environments. You benefit from the luck of allies but this does not mean you don't have rivals. Don't make yourself vulnerable to criticism. Get to work on time, don't make it a habit to leave work early, and most importantly, get the job done. If you have targets to meet, these are likely to be scrutinized more closely this month. You get some respite next month, but this is a time when there is little room for error and mistakes have a tendency to get magnified. Wear a **mantra ring** to control the bristly energy of the month and to tap on divine help. The **Rooster** is also a good feng shui symbol to invest in this month, as it will protect you against workplace politics.

BUSINESS - *Stay Careful*

The misfortune star of the year gets magnified this month, so it is prudent to stay careful. Don't expose yourself to unnecessary risk. This is not a good time to cut deals or sign agreements. Maintain the status quo if things are going well. Don't try anything new. Moving into unchartered territory is asking for trouble. Even if you have exciting plans in the pipeline, hold on till next month if you can. Your personal luck improves tremendously then, and if you are helming your organization, it is best to take heed of your auspicious and inauspicious months. This is a time for you to lie low. Avoid taking too high a profile. Next month things improve and you can be more flamboyant if you wish.

LOVE & RELATIONSHIPS - *Sizzling!*

Relationships heat up this month and you're sizzling with passion. While you may be tentative when it comes to work, business and deal making, your love life is a different ballgame altogether! You are on form! You find yourself extremely attractive to others this month, and turning on the charm is no problem for you. Just be yourself and you'll attract yourself a lot of suitors. But if you're thinking of entering into something more serious, it may be better to wait till next month. Keep things fun and frivolous and you're likely to enjoy it more that way. Don't commit to things you are not ready for or you could find it difficult to back out later.

EDUCATION - *Focus Your Energies*

Since your luck is not great this month, try not to take on too much. Continue working conscientiously, but don't go out on a limb to be popular or to be a martyr helping out all your classmates. If you don't focus your energies you may find you do surprisingly badly, even in subjects you are usually good at.

8TH MONTH
Sept 8th - Oct 7th 2011

DETERMINATION BRINGS POSITIVE RESULTS

This is a month when hard work certainly pays off. Money and success luck comes your way, but it is not without a hard slog. This will be a physically and mentally exhausting period, but there is much to be gained. Business luck is good, especially for those of you who take a long-term approach. Forget short-term profits and aim for something that can last and you won't go wrong. The main problem for you this month is tiredness and succumbing to exhaustion. As long as you keep yourself healthy, you should come out of the month better than you started it. For Rabbits climbing the career ladder, there is promotion luck on the cards. For those of you in business, take advantage of your material luck this month. This may not be the time to take big risks, but it is a time when gritting your teeth and grinding out the work will pay off.

WORK & CAREER - *Promotion Luck*

If you are looking to climb the career ladder, this is a month when getting to the next rung is a possibility.

Your leadership qualities are enhanced this month, so if you are in a supervisory or managerial role, use your position to get the most out of your staff. Do not just dish out work; treat your subordinates like team members to increase productivity in your department. What could be your undoing is stress and exhaustion. The more productive and into your job you get, the more pressure you will feel. Allocate some quiet time each day to lower your blood pressure, or your health may suffer.

BUSINESS - *Growth and Expansion*

Rabbits in business benefit from wealth and success luck this month. There are many opportunities to expand your business. However, you will find that you cannot do everything yourself. This may be the time to bring in some new people to join your team and to help you grow and expand. Unless you invest in additional manpower, you could find it very difficult to gain from opportunities that are opening up to you. There may also be someone in your staff you have been considering elevating to status of partner. This could well be the time to do this.

LOVE & RELATIONSHIPS - *Be More Giving*

Try not to be over-controlling in your relationships. Your need for your partner to conform to how you believe they should be won't earn you points in the passion stakes. Resist the temptation to lecture and instead treat your partner like a true equal. It is never nice to be talked down to, so don't do it to the one person you're supposed to care about the most. Focus on your partner's needs instead of your own and you'll find more happiness than you would have imagined. A fabulous month for love and relationships as long as you play your cards right.

EDUCATION - *Ambition Pays Off*

A fabulous month lies ahead for the Rabbit in school. Knowledge sticks and you find your mind in sharp and easy focus. Things become clear and you truly begin to enjoy your studies. Months like these should not go to waste. Put more effort into your schoolwork and you can become a real star this month. This could be a breakthrough period where you jump to the next level of achievement. Make the most of your ambitious streak this month and give everything a go. You may not be good at everything you try your hand at, but practice makes perfect, and if you never try, you'll never know.

9TH MONTH
Oct 8th - Nov 6th 2011

BE CAREFUL
NOT TO GET CONNED THIS MONTH

This month brings all kinds of danger. You could suffer from financial loss either through being robbed, cheated or betrayed. You really should place feng shui remedies in place this month if you're to dodge the loss star in your chart. Get a **double horned rhino and a six tusk elephant**, and place in the East part of your home. It is also good idea to carry as an amulet. Avoid getting into fights because you're likely to come out on the losing end. Try to find amicable solutions to everything. It is much better that way. Troublemakers could enter your life, bringing provocation and aggravations. Lie low and abstain from retaliating. The hostile winds blow away next month, so just sit tight and hold on till then.

WORK & CAREER - *Office Politics*

Although your fortunes do not bode well this month, you have the luck of resources and energy. Use your energy reserves to out-manipulate those who choose to take you on, and make sure you are surrounded by allies you can trust. Don't fall into the trap of opening up to someone you don't know too well, especially when it comes to someone at work, for they may well use your woes against you. You could also find yourself falling victim to office politics this month. There is an indication of troublemakers in your chart, so it is important to stay alert. It is vital to maintain the support of your boss or you could find yourself being politicked out of the picture. Carry the **Double Ring Magic Fire Wheel Amulet** to protect yourself this month.

BUSINESS - *Avoid Risk Taking*

Although this is not the month to dream up grand projects or be overly ambitious, there is no harm in conceptualizing your thoughts. Thinking never caused anyone any harm, but because this is a bad month, even thoughts have a way of turning unlucky. So it is best to avoid taking any big risks or making major decisions this month. Keep a watch internally also; there could be a defector or spy in the office. While you shouldn't become paranoid, it is probably wise to be a bit more careful with sensitive information and internal security.

Carry the **Double Ring Magic Fire Wheel amulet** to protect against office politics and gossip.

LOVE & RELATIONSHIPS - *Mistrust*

There could be a sense of mistrust when it comes to your love life this month. But even if you suspect your partner is hiding something from you, it is probably better to avoid a confrontation and let skeletons stay in the closet. Having it out this month is not going to be good for either of you. This is a stressful month for relationships, and if you value your relationship, carry or wear the double happiness symbol with you at all times, and try and get your partner to do the same. This will help you weather the bad times smoothly and successfully.

EDUCATION - *Stay Out Of Trouble*

Schoolwork may not be so enjoyable this month. There may be more work than usual and your ability to get into your teachers' good books may have evaporated for the time being. Stay out of trouble by ensuring you don't inadvertently break any school rules. This may be a month when you may get yourself caught. This could also be a time when you find out who your real friends are.

10TH MONTH
Nov 7th - Dec 6th 2011

MENTORING LUCK
BRINGS HELPFUL ASSISTANCE

This is a lucky month for you when you are blessed with luck from above. New opportunities open up fresh directions for you and these have the potential to help you change career path or to enhance your business. How you profit from your good luck will depend on your brainpower as well as your attitude towards your goals. Those of you who stay focused and determined will do well, while those who prefer to trundle along won't stumble upon any misfortune but will not shine either.

WORK & CAREER - *Get the Support of the Boss*

Getting ahead in the career game can be more stressful than you think, especially if you work in a high-paced and highly competitive environment. Sometimes being the most hardworking or even the best at what you do isn't enough. This is when you need to employ other methods to get ahead. If you are uncomfortable playing the part of the political animal, don't. But make sure you have your boss and superiors firmly on your side. The way to tap into your good mentor luck this month is to ensure you sit with a solid wall behind you; even better if you can hang or place an **image of a mountain** behind you. This will ensure you get all the support you need from the right quarters.

BUSINESS - *Help from Unexpected Quarters*

Exciting opportunities open up for you this month. Consider them all but try not to get carried away. You may have to put your full concentration on one or two things rather than jumping the gun and getting yourself into more than you can handle. Be sharp in your thinking and strategize before making hasty decisions. Your luck is good this month and help can come from unexpected quarters. Open your mind to new and progressive ways of doing things, and don't shoot down ideas just because they don't at first appear that promising. You could be pleasantly surprised.

LOVE & RELATIONSHIPS - *Lucky in Love*

This is a lucky month for Rabbits looking for love. Romance is in the air and could come in a form most unexpected. Open your mind and your heart and let yourself be swept off your feet. If you learn to relax and go with the flow, you could finally meet someone who really catches your heart.

For those of you who are married, this is a good month to jazz things up a little. Particularly if you are the male in the relationship, make an effort this month to surprise your spouse with simple, romantic gestures to rekindle the passion in your marriage. It may even take your relationship to a new and deeper level.

EDUCATION - *Mentor Luck*

This month sees someone older watching over you. You will find a mentor who will be beneficial for you. You should feel very privileged with this lucky development. This person will help you with good advice and counsel and will continue to help you if you let them.

11TH MONTH
Dec 7th - Jan 5th 2012

A MONTH OF SETBACKS

This is a dangerous month for the Rabbit-born, with a concentration of misfortune stars in your chart. It is vital that you be very careful this month in all areas of your life. Do not take risks as you are in danger of losing big money. Do not wander dark streets at night and make sure you have the security at your home looked over; there is danger of robbery and break-ins. Avoid yin dwellings such as graveyards and prisons, for the unfortunate Chi of such places may combine with your personal bad luck to manifest misfortune. Wear plenty of gold jewellery as well as the powerful **mystic knot symbol**, which will protect you against harm as well as prompt auspicious things to materialize in your life. Better to stay home than to go out too much.

The Auspicious **mystic knot** symbol

WORK & CAREER - *A Mixed Month*

This is a mixed month when it comes to work and working life. There may be some strong conflicts of opinion in the workplace that involve yourself, but standing your ground is likely to pay off. Don't expect smooth sailing in the office this month; it will certainly be a bumpy ride, but one that is ultimately fulfilling. While you have the double misfortune star in your chart, you also enjoy completion luck, especially if you are tenacious and determined. The perfectionist in the Rabbit personality will serve you well this month. Don't let any stone go unturned; while obstacles and setbacks may present some hiccups along the way, by month end, any problems that arise will happily sort themselves out.

BUSINESS - *Stick to Familiar Ground*

This month is best tackled quietly. Lie low and stick to familiar ground. Avoid risky ventures as misfortune stars are hovering nearby waiting to play havoc with your prospects. As well as providence not being on your side, your energy levels are also being sapped and you may not be as sharp or ready to react as you usually are. Don't enter into important negotiations this month. If there are serious matters to resolve with regards to your business, it is better to send your partner or assistant than deal with it personally.

Rabbits who work well with others will do better than soloists this month.

LOVE & RELATIONSHIPS - *Don't expect too much*

Luck in love is poorly this month, so forget about finding your perfect soul mate for now. You may be feeling rejected or let down if a love interest has recently given you the cold shoulder. Don't expect too much when it comes to romance and passion this month or you'll only be disappointed. This is a time to reflect inward. Your time is better spent at home curled up with a book than trying to play the dating game.

Married Rabbits have it better than their single counterparts this month. In fact, if you have a good relationship with your partner, you will find them a great source of moral support this month.

EDUCATION - *Work Hard*

While luck in general is not super this month, the young Rabbit should continue to work hard and keep striving for good results. When things are difficult, you should double your efforts and try even harder. Don't let your grades slip or it could become a habit. Put in more effort and time into your schoolwork and you could come out of the month even better than you entered it.

needs to be quelled with a **Flaming Magic Wheel** placed in the SW sector. Enhance your personal romance luck with a Rat in the North of your bedroom. When dating, don't take yourself too seriously. Let loose a little and you'll find yourself enjoying yourself a lot! Married Rabbits should beware the romantic star, as this can be a double-edged sword. Pay more attention to your spouse and romance can be rekindled in the most brilliant way, but if you're both too busy leading your own lives, there is some danger of infidelity this month. It is advisable to wear a **Rooster with Amethyst and Fan** as a safeguard for your marriage.

EDUCATION - *Exam Luck is Excellent*

Study luck is promising for the young Rabbit, so make the best use of this month to learn new things. Put more effort into your assignments and make a decided effort to improve the level of your work. This is also a good time to develop your relationships with your teachers. Get close to them if you can. They can be of a lot more help if you bother to dig deeper. Exam luck is excellent so those of you sitting for tests and exams this month can rest assured the stars are on your side.

Important Feng Shui Updates for 2011

Part 6

If you have been following the advice given in these Fortune & Feng Shui books on annual feng shui updates, you are already familiar with the time dimension of feng shui which protects against negative luck each year.

This requires overall cleansing and re-energizing of the energy of the home to prepare for the coming of a new year, while simultaneously making placement changes to accommodate a new pattern of chi distribution. Getting rid of old items and replacing with specially made new remedial cures that are in tune with the year's chi brings pristine and fresh new luck into the home.

It is truly vital to anticipate and quickly suppress the source of malicious chi brought by the year's new feng shui winds as this ensures that bad chi born in afflicted sectors never have a chance to gather, accumulate, grow strong and then ripen in a burst of bad luck! With powerful remedies in place, this will not happen, thereby keeping residents safe from the kind of harm that can be unsettling and heartbreaking.

Severe bad luck can happen to anyone; sometimes, even in the midst of some personal triumphant moment, your world can suddenly crumble. Last year for instance, the world witnessed the incredibly sad falling apart of the marriages of **Kate Winslet** and **Sandra Bullock** soon after they each had reached the pinnacle of their profession by winning the Oscar for Best Actress.

Kate had won in 2009 and Sandra in 2010. Both had breathlessly thanked their husbands obviously unaware of destructive energies lurking within their homes. Both husbands - for whatever reasons - were looking for gratification outside their marriages! Kate's husband, noted Director Sam Mendes' eyes had already started roving in 2009... but the marriage fell apart in 2010 when the star of infidelity made its appearance.

Both actresses do not believe in luck… it is safe to assume they are too busy to arrange for the placement of feng shui cures in their homes.

Those not following time dimension feng shui from these books are unlikely to have known that last year 2010 was a year when the *external romance star of peach blossom* was lurking in every household, creating the potential to cause havoc in marriages! It was vital last year to place cures in the home to protect against outsider third party interference. Sandra Bullock and Kate Winslet are just two of the high profile victims of the star of *External Peach Blossom*! They are exquisitely beautiful ladies, but both of their marriages unraveled in March of 2010!

It is therefore so important that each time we cross into a new year, we should note the particular ailments and afflictions of the year, and then carefully bring in the antidotes so we can sail through the year without having to endure the consequences of bad feng shui, which of course can manifest in different ways. No matter how it manifests, bad luck always brings distress, heartbreak and a sense of helplessness.

Why go through this kind of unhappiness when you can prevent or reduce it?

Each year there will be the same kinds of afflictions bringing illness, accidents, robbery, quarrels and severe misfortune, but these afflictions change location each year and vary in strength from year to year. So we need to systematically suppress these "*staples of bad luck*" first.

Then there are the disturbing stars of misfortune - these too need to be neutralized mainly with element therapy so that they do not cast their ill influence onto your luck. In some years, there can be some hazardous or dangerous alignment of energies we need to be careful of, and these also need to be addressed. For instance, we have already told you about the four pillars of clashing elements bringing severe quarrelsome energy that can get violent.

It is SO vital for everyone but especially for the Rabbit-born to be alert to dangers in the bigger picture. This is a year when you need to make a concerted effort to protect yourself as you are directly afflicted by the five yellow flying into your home location of East. You must place the **Five Element Pagoda** with the **Tree of Life** on your East sectors to safeguard your house energy and everyone in it from getting hit by the five yellow affliction.

Using Incense

To overcome the overriding disharmonious energies of the year, one effective way to prevent your family being negatively affected is to use incense as a way of dispelling all the bad energy. Incense is a powerful way of transcending time and space, blending heaven and earth energies to chase away all the afflictions that bring disaster, setbacks and accidents. In fact, incense and scents, although invisible, are such a powerful way of overcoming obstacles that they have been used by all the major traditions of the world.

The use of incense is one of the most powerful ways of overcoming all kinds of obstacles that may be blocking your luck. The use of incense is part of spiritual feng shui - the third dimension of inner feng shui that can make such a difference to really allowing great good fortune into your life.

The use of incense is one of the most powerful ways to overcome obstacles in your life.

This is because creating a regular infusion of incense (with some smoke) works incredibly well for clearing the pathway for good chi energy to flow into your home; and with empowering symbolic placements, these work together to create the lucky ambience you need.

Home energy then becomes harmonious and benevolent, blending beautifully with new patterns of chi formations that are flowing through your home. Just try infusing your space with the special blend of sandalwood or pine incense and feel the difference instantly!

Focusing on your house feng shui from this perspective will help you enjoy a better year irrespective of how good or how bad the indications for the year may be. This is because the correct kind of aromas can go a long way to subduing the afflictions in all the afflicted corners of the house, hence protecting everyone in the household.

Misfortune is always worse and have nastier consequences when they creep up on you. These come in many ways, for instance, when confronted with the prospect of losing your job, your home, your good name, your child, your lover or your spouse.

It is only when afflictive energies are suppressed that bad happenings become manageable. They can even be avoided. This is the wonderful promise and benefit of creating good and timely feng shui in the home.

And when divine assistance is invoked through the wearing of powerful amulets and sacred talismans, the remedies become even more effective. This brings harmony and smooth sailing through the year.

Luck is Never Static

Luck always occurs in cycles and the key to continuing good fortune is to know when the luck of your house is at its peak and when it requires extra protection. When important parts of the house you live in get hit by misfortune-bringing stars, everyone living within gets hurt.

In the same way, when these same areas are visited by lucky stars, everyone in the house enjoys good fortune. To what degree this incidence of good and bad luck affects residents depends also on their personal outlook for the year. Cycles of luck affect different people in different ways and this is one reason why it is so beneficial to analyze how the year affects your animal sign.

Consider the infinite variations of each individual's pattern of luck when you factor in the two sets of elements in the four sets of birth data - Year, Month, Day and Hour of Birth... then factor in the house, locations of the main door, bedroom, dining and living area. Factor in also the changing energies of the year, as well as the energy of the people who surround you, who make up your circle of family and friends... and you will be awed by the mathematical combinations of chi that are affecting you every single moment!

We cannot take care of everything that affects our luck, but we sure can take care of enough to ensure a pretty good and smooth year. And once we are assured that we have been adequately protected against sudden misfortunes, we can then turn our attention to maximizing and magnifying good fortune for the year... Success, Love, Satisfaction with Life, Money, Wealth, Career highs, Contentment... and a lot more can then be induced to manifest into our lives.

This depends on what we want, what we energize for and how we enhance our bedrooms, work spaces and living areas. It is really easier than you think! Just protect against bad luck and energize for good luck.

You must first protect your **main door** and your **bedroom**. The location of these two important parts of your house must be protected against bad numbers or bad stars. Afflictive energy can be illness or misfortune numbers, hostile or robbery stars. These can, together with other kinds of negative energy, cause loss of some kind. Someone might force you into litigation - this is something that will happen more than normal this year; or you might suffer a break-up of an important relationship - this too is unfortunately being fanned by the destructive patterns of elements this year.

Severe bad luck or loss, when it manifests, is always traumatic. Feng shui corrections offer the solutions to avoiding or at least diminishing negativities happening. Knowing feng shui enables you to anticipate a potentially problematic year; and then to do something about it.

Correcting and suppressing bad energy is rarely difficult. But it requires a bit of effort. What you must do is systematically go through each of the nine sectors of your home, mentally dividing each level of your home into a three by three sector grid that corresponds to eight compass directions with a center.

The next step is to study the year's charts; first, the Annual Feng Shui chart which pinpoints the afflicted parts of the home, then the 24 mountain charts which show the "stars", both lucky and unlucky, that also influence the year's distribution of luck, and finally, the year's four pillars chart. It is the collective and unified analysis of these indications that point to what needs to be done to safeguard the feng shui of any abode.

Suppressing Flying Star Afflictions for the Year

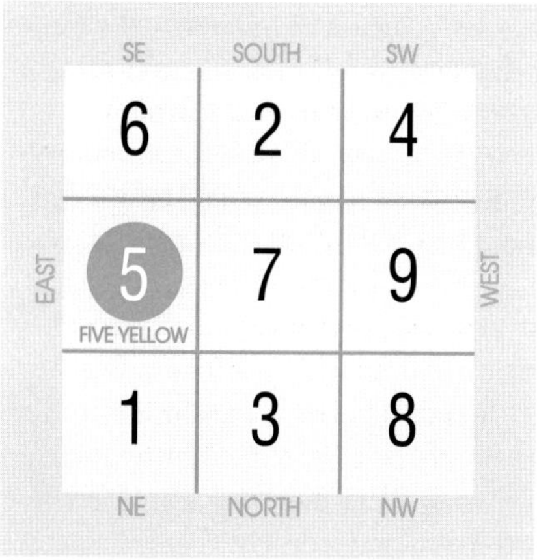
SE
SOUTH
SW
6
2
4
EAST
5
FIVE YELLOW
7
9
WEST
1
3
8
NE
NORTH
NW

Traditionally, one of the more important things to update prior to each new year is to find the new locations for all the afflictive star numbers and then to deal with each of them. These yearly afflictions are the same each year, but their strength and severity vary from year to year, depending on where they are. The element of each affliction interacts with the element of the sector they fly into. In some years for instance, the misfortune star number of five yellow a.k.a. **wu wang** can be really strong, while in some years it is weaker.

In 2011, for instance, the *wu wang* flies to the East, where its Earth element is strongly suppressed by the Wood element here. The 2011 *wu wang* is thus not as strong as it was in the previous year when it occupied the Southwest. There, the Earth element of the Southwest strengthened the *wu wang*. In 2011 therefore we are not so afraid of this otherwise feared star. In spite of this it is still advisable to keep the *wu wang* under control in case someone in the house is going through weak Life Force year or whose Spirit Essence may be lacking. The East is the home location of the Rabbit so the wu wang hurts the Rabbit more than anyone else; it is true that the Rabbit's Wood element can overcome the *wu wang*, so it is less of a threat than it normally is.

Remedies against the Wu Wang

But it is still necessary to place the traditional remedies to suppress *wu wang* in the East because it is a thoroughly unpleasant star number whose effect could suddenly manifest; and even those who are not born Rabbits, but whose bedroom happens to be here, they are also affected by it, especially if the East sector is also being hit by some secret unknown poison arrow; this can act as a catalyst for the *wu wang* to erupt, or when the Wood element here gets inadvertently weakened for whatever reason.

The *wu wang* blocks success and it affects the luck of the eldest son of the family. So to be safe, get the cures that have been specially designed for the year and place these in the East sectors. Do not forget the East walls of your important rooms and also the living and family areas where you and your family spend a great deal of time. Place the cures on a sideboard or table, not on the floor!

Five Element Pagoda with Tree of Life

In 2011 we are recommending the five element pagoda that comes with a wood base and is decorated with an all-powerful Tree of Life that grows from the base of the pagoda right to the tip. There are three pairs of birds on the branches of the tree of life.

These birds bring opportunities from the cosmic constellations and legend has it they attract exactly the kind of luck a household needs. From the leaves of the tree hang glittering jewels which signify the treasures of the earth, the element that symbolizes wealth and prosperity in 2011.

This powerful five element pagoda is actually a transforming tool which turns the all powerful wu wang into a wealth enhancing tool. It greatly benefits the Rabbit in 2011 who will gain enormously from this symbol of protection. Note that this particular pagoda with the tree of life synchronizes extremely well with the energies of 2011 and 2012 when the *wu wang* flies to the Wood sectors of the compass.

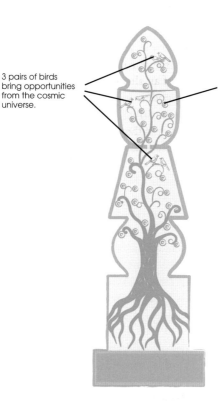

3 pairs of birds bring opportunities from the cosmic universe.

Jewels hanging from the tree branches symbolizes Earth, the element of prosperity in 2011.

The **five element pagoda** with Tree of Life transforms the wu wang into a wealth-bringing star.

Metal Bell with Tree of Life

Another very beneficial cure for the 2011 *wu wang* is the powerful Bell which is also made of metal but has a wooden mallet so the sound created is mellower and lower than that of an all-metal bell. The handle of the bell is made of wood; and on the bell itself there is again the amazing tree of life to strengthen the wood chi of the East; and the tree also has 6 birds on its branches; and with jewels on its leaves to signify wealth luck.

The **Metal Bell** with wooden handle is another enhancing tool that simultaneously suppresses the wu wang.

This transforms the five element bell into an empowering, enhancing tool which, even as it suppresses the *wu wang*, is simultaneously sending out powerful vibrations each time the sounds of the bell are created. This way the bell utilizes the wu wang to attract great good fortune opportunities and it is by placing a tree of life with 6 birds that gives it these attributes. We have also embossed the *dependent arising mantra* onto both the five element bell and pagoda. This powerful mantra greatly empowers these cures!

Those wanting to wear these powerful symbols over the two years 2011 and 2012 can consider wearing either the pagoda or the bell with the tree design to safeguard themselves from the *wu wang*.

Those of you born in the Rabbit year you must be extra careful in the month of **March** and **December** as this is the month when the wu wang flies into your month chart, strengthening it considerably.

Misfortunes caused by the *wu wang* in 2011 are not as severe as in other years, but they are nonetheless annoying and aggravating. It can cause problems with employees or act as a catalyst for other kinds of bad luck to erupt, so it is a good idea to suppress its negative effect. This year's cure does just that but it also uses the inherent strength of the *wu wang* to transform bad luck into something good.

If you reside in a room located in the East sector of your house, place the pagoda inside your bedroom. Make sure it is in place before February 3rd which is the start of the Lunar New Year 2011. It is also important to take note that there should not be any renovations done in the East side of the house through 2011.

Avoid all kinds of demolition or digging work although there are some feng shui masters who say that building works are not harmful, arguing that anything productive will not harm the household. We disagree with this as the *wu wang* should not be activated by any kind of building. This only strengthens it. Planting a tree in the East is however auspicious, especially if you do this on February 4th the day of the *lap chun*!

Planting a tree on the **4th February,** the day of the **Lap Chun**, is extremely auspicious!

OTHER AFFLICTIONS
OF THE 2011 CHART
The Illness Star flies to the South in 2011

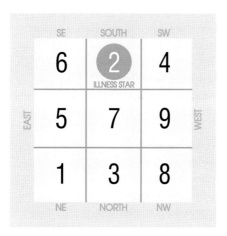

SE	SOUTH	SW
6	2 ILLNESS STAR	4
5	7	9
1	3	8
NE	NORTH	NW

This is an Earth element star flying into a Fire sector, so here, the illness star gets considerably strengthened, making it a serious threat to residents, but especially for anyone residing in the South sector of the house; but the illness star affects everyone if it is where the main door into the house is located. Any house that faces or sits South will find that residents within are more vulnerable to catching viruses and falling ill more easily.

Should the main door of the house be in the South, the constant opening and closing of the door will energize the star making it more likely to bring illness into the house and this is pronounced during the months of March and December when the month stars mirror that of the year hence bringing a double whammy to afflicted sectors.

If your door is facing South, it is a good idea to use another door located in another sector (if possible) especially during these two months. If this is not possible then it is necessary to exhaust the Earth element of the illness star placing something metallic or made of wood here. It is necessary also to remove all earth element items such as crystals, porcelain vases or stone objects. Also keep lights in the South dim to reduce Fire element energy.

Many popular deities such as **Kwan Yin carry the Wu Lou**, which generates invisible healing energies.

Cures for the Illness Star of 2011

Over the years we have found the best way to suppress illness energy brought by the intangible flying star 2 is with a **wu lou** shaped container made of metal - either in brass or steel. The wu lou is a container for keeping herbal cures so that over the years it has come to signify medicinal qualities. Many popular deities such as the **Goddess of Mercy**, Kuan Yin, carry a small wu lou shaped little bottle that contains healing nectar. Placing a **large wu lou** in the South generates invisible healing energies for both physical and mental afflictions. It is an excellent idea to place a small wu lou by your bedside so that it exudes healing energies as you sleep. This is good feng shui!

Wear the watch with the healing image of Medicine Buddha if you are feeling poorly.

You can also invoke the help of the powerful healing Buddha, also known as the **Medicine Buddha**. This is the blue Buddha who create enormous blessings in any home that displays his image or mantra in any way at all, especially in the sector where the flying illness star is located. The Medicine Buddha ensures that all residents enjoy good health, rarely if ever falling sick. It is a good idea in 2011 to have an image of the Medicine Buddha placed on a table top in the North part of any room where you spend time.

Those feeling poorly in 2011 should also wear **Medicine Buddha bracelets** or our specially designed **moving mantra watches** - the only watches of its kind in the world! We brought out the first such moving mantra watch last year and they have since helped so many people that we have extended our range to include a watch with the healing image of the Medicine Buddha.

Wearing such a watch is like having prayers being constantly recited for your good health. It is truly amazing how far technology has progressed. To us, it makes sense to utilize all the technical advances that have made so many wonderful new products possible. Many of the advances in technology have made feng shui very easy to practice.

The Quarrelsome Hostile Star flies to the North in 2011

This is a Wood element star flying into a Water element sector. As such this noisy, litigation bringing star number is both strong and harder to overcome. It is dangerous and aggravating and very capable of causing anyone staying in the North sector a great deal of problems.

This is the major affliction affecting the North sector in 2011. There is stress which could well affect your productivity and for some of you can even be the cause of delay and obstacles. At its worst, the effect of this affliction is someone taking you to court, causing you aggravations and inconvenience. Someone whose room is here might also get violent.

This star brings a pervasive feeling of hostility, short tolerance levels and a great deal of impatience. There will be arguments, fights and misunderstandings for everyone directly hit by it.

Unfortunately for anyone having a bedroom in the North sector of the house, the quarrelsome star 3 is made stronger this year because its Wood Element is produced even more by the Water element of the North. As a Wood element star, the best way to subdue its effect is to exhaust it with Fire Element energy. Anything that suggests Fire is an excellent cure, so bright lights and the color red are excellent remedies. Hence, because the North is associated with Water energy, the danger is enhanced, so remedying it is vital.

An excellent cure against the 3 star is the **Red Dragon amulet**. This brings luck while keeping the number 3 star subdued. It is excellent for anyone having their bedroom in the North or those living in homes with main doors that face North. Note that this amulet has the Dragon carrying a sword in its right claw as this helps overcome all the clashing elements of the year.

The Violent Star 7
attracts bad people into the home

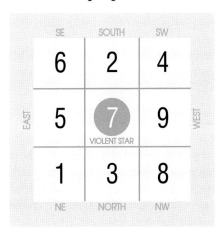

The Violent star 7 is in the center of the chart this year, where it is symbolically locked up, hence reducing its influence. This is an affliction which hurts most when it occupies one of the outer sectors of any building, but trapped in the center, its negative impact is less severe.

The number 7 star number is an Metal element number and with the center being an Earth sector, here we have a situation of Earth producing Metal, so while it may *be hemmed in in the center, it is nevertheless troublesome. It is a number that causes loss through being cheated or robbed.*

A good way of keeping this affliction under wraps is simply to place a small sideboard in the center of the house, place seven pieces of metal within and then lock it up. This symbolically "locks up" the number 7 star very effectively. At the same time, have a **Rhino with an Elephant** near the entrance into the home.

However, should any of you be feeling vulnerable with the burglary star in the center of the home, you can safeguard yourself by carrying the **blue-colored Rhino** or using it as a hanging on your bags or hung in the car. It is good practice to stay protected against encountering bad people who would want to harm you. Use the **Blue Rhino protector** as this continues to be an effective cure in 2011. It is a highly respected cure against the potential violence of the 7.

Note that the problem with the number 7 star in 2011 is that being in the center of the feng shui chart, the number 7 can potentially spread its influence into any part of the house, hence it is necessary to keep it well under control. The best is to literally "*lock it up*", otherwise it simply plays havoc with house security. It is very inconvenient and even dangerous when the 7 star number strikes.

In 2011 the God of the Year cannot be ignored

The Tai Sui is important because this year, it directly faces the *star of natural disaster* in the West sector of the chart. This is a 24 mountain star that sits between the two stars of *three killings*! That there are such intensive negative stars directly confronting the Tai Sui is not good for the year. It suggests a battle, and when a battle takes place, there is always collateral damage!

Especially when they are read against the background of the year's clashing elements in the four pillars, these signs collectively indicate clear and present danger. How the dangers of the year manifest will vary in timing and severity for different houses and different countries; but generally, an afflicted Tai Sui means that the wars of the world currently being waged on several fronts are unlikely to decline. There is also no let up in the occurrence of natural disasters. It is therefore important to be extra mindful of the Tai Sui in 2011. Avoid confronting it. Avoid facing East and make extra efforts not to "*disturb*" its location, the East sector of the house. This sector must be kept quiet as noise activates the Tai Sui and incurs its wrath. Also avoid digging, banging or renovating this side of the home.

The Rabbit is supported by the Tai Sui, and is unlikely to be hurt by it but because it is a Tai Sui that is hurt by the disaster star opposite, it is advisable for the Rabbit born to use Tai Sui amulets as a measure of protection. The 2011 Tai Sui resides in the East, the home location of the Rabbit; but this year's Tai Sui is not as benevolent as the previous year, so it is good to be mindful. Observe all the taboos associated with Tai Sui. No digging, banging, cutting and definitely no renovations to this part of the house.

It is beneficial to place a well-executed art piece of the beautiful **Pi Yao** in the East, as this celestial creature appeases the Tai Sui. The Pi Yao brings good feng shui. You can find many artistic variations of this auspicious creature all over China and Hong Kong. It is a great favorite with people who believe in feng shui as it brings exceptional good fortune into the home. For 2011, a Pi Yao made in Earth element material is preferred as this element signifies wealth luck. So crystal or ceramic Pi Yao, or one made in liu li, would be excellent.

It is important for everyone whose bedroom is in the East, or whose sitting direction while working is facing or sitting East, to place the Pi Yao near you;

It does not matter if the Pi Yao is standing or sitting but it should appear proud and majestic looking. The more beautiful looking the Pi Yao is the better it is to display in the house to appease the Tai Sui. *This advice applies to anyone irrespective of their animal sign.*

The place of the Tai Sui is taken very seriously in feng shui. It is emphasized in the Treatise on Harmonizing Times and Distinguishing Directions compiled under the patronage of the Qianlong Emperor during his reign in the mid Eighteenth century and any Master practicing feng shui in China or Hong Kong always ensures the Tai Sui is respected and thus taken account of in their updating process.

The Emperor Qiang Lung inspired Treatise states that the locations where the Tai Sui resides and where the Tai Sui has just vacated are **lucky** locations. So note that in 2011, the locations of East and Northeast 1 are considered lucky benefiting from the lingering energy of the Tai Sui. Those having their rooms in these two locations will enjoy the patronage and protection of the Tai Sui in 2011.

The Treatise further explains that it is **unlucky** to reside in the location where the Tai Sui is progressing towards i.e. clockwise on the astrology compass.

In 2011 this means the Southeast 1 location; it is unlucky to directly confront the Tai Sui's residence. It is unlucky to "*face*" the Tai Sui because this is deemed rude, so the advice for 2011 is to not to directly face East.

In 2011, never forget to avoid confronting the Tai Sui. Do not face East this year even if this is your success direction under the Kua formula of personalized lucky directions. Those who forget and inadvertently face the Tai Sui run the risk of offending the Tai Sui. This brings obstacles to your work life. Your road to achieving success gets constantly interrupted and for some, supporters can turn into adversaries.

Place a **Pi Yao** in the East sector of the home this year to appease the Tai Sui who resides there in 2011.

The Tai Sui Amulet for 2011.

Part 6 : Important Feng Shui Updates for 2011

In 2011 the West of every building is afflicted by the Three Killings

This affliction brings three severe misfortunes associated with loss, grief and sadness. Its location each year is charted according to the animal sign that rules the year. Thus in 2011 it flies to the West because the Rabbit belongs to the Triangle of Affinity made up of the Rabbit, Sheep and Boar; with the Rabbit occupying a cardinal direction (East).

The Three Killings is thus in the West, the direction that is directly opposite the Rabbit. This feng shui aggravation affects only primary directions, so unlike other feng shui afflictions, the direct bad effects of the *three killings* are felt over a larger area of the house.

When you suffer a sudden reversal of fortune, it is usually due to being hit by the three killings. In 2011 the *three killings* resides in the West, where it poses some danger to the young daughters of the family. Anyone occupying the West would be vulnerable to being hit by the *three killings*.

For everyone whose bedroom and/or main doors face West or are located in the West sector of your home, please get the **celestial protectors** - the Chi lin, Fu Dog and Pi Yao - preferably made colorful and with a fierce expression. Place them together on a coffee table or sideboard; get them in brass and enamel.

For them to be effective, some texts refer also to the three different deities traditionally seated on their backs, but as a feng shui cure, they are as effective on their own or with the deities, although the secret is to make sure they have their different **implements** with them, as these enable them to symbolically overcome the afflictions.

Thus the **Sword** on the back of the **Pi Yao** protects against loss of wealth. The **Lasso** on the back of the **Chi Lin** to protects against loss of loved one. The **steel hook** on the back of the **Fu Dog** protects against loss of good name. The hook is a very powerful implement which also "hooks in wealth luck".

These three celestial guardians are extremely effective; but this year an old Taoist master has advised to also add in the implements; he confirmed that as feng shui cures, they work best when they are new. This ensures that their energy is strong. Do not use antique images as feng shui cures as these are usually surrounded by tired chi. It is important that feng shui remedies have fresh energy so there is strong vigor and vitality chi attached to them. Antique furniture decorated with celestials can be lovely to look at, but they rarely make powerful cures.

They can however generate auspicious chi after they are cleansed of lingering yin vibes. Use a dry cloth with either sea salt or crystal salt to wipe off stale chi and they should be fine. Do this cleansing ritual at least once a year. The month before the lunar new year is a good time.

The energy of the *three killings* can sometimes stick onto furniture, especially those with animals or human images painted onto them. It is a good idea to use raw salt as a way of wiping off lingering bad chi. Those of who may want to stay protected from the *three killings* and prevent them from overwhelming you when you are out and about this year can also hang the **three celestials amulet** on your hand bags and pocket books. Those of you staying in the West sectors of the house, you could experience bad dreams and nightmares and if so, make sure you place the **three celestial guardians** on a cabinet along the West wall of the room. If you have a window in the bedroom, place the three celestials there even if it is not the West wall. The presence of the three guardians is a powerful cosmic force that protects.

Display the **3 celestial protectors** in the West to counter the 3 Killings affliction in 2011. It is even better when these protectors carry the implements of the Deities they are associated with, as these enable them to effectively overcome the afflictions.

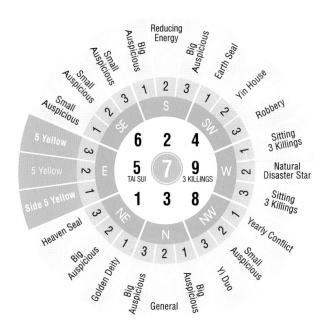

Rabbit is afflicted by the 5 Yellow in 2011

Subduing the Left and Right of Rabbit's Luck

The Rabbit is seriously afflicted by the stars of the 24 mountains in 2011 on both its left and right as the East locations are all playing host to the five yellow (*wu wang*). This reflects the number 5 flying into the East sector in the flying star chart. To subdue the 24 mountain stars of five yellow, you must place the five element pagoda with the tree of life here. Remember that placement feng shui works best when there is accuracy of compass readings, so it is a good idea to invest in a good compass and to learn to take accurate compass readings.

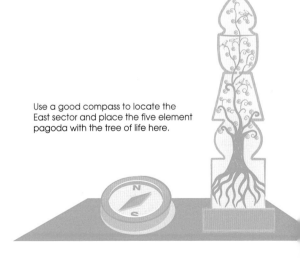

Use a good compass to locate the East sector and place the five element pagoda with the tree of life here.

Suppressing Anger Vibrations in the North

We have already noted that the North is the sector where the angry star 3 has flown to in 2011. This can be suppressed by using the **Red Dragon amulet**. Anger vibrations are what will cause problems for anyone residing in the North as this will block the manifestation of good fortune.

One of the best ways to prevent anger vibrations getting out of hand is to use two powerful rituals, both using the medium of incense. Scents, aromas, incense - these are powerful mediums that can transcend the cosmic fields of energy that affect us.

We have spent the past year talking about the third dimension of feng shui, and the use of aromatic incense is one of the more common ways used by Masters skilled in the shamanistic aspects of feng shui practice. At its most basic, joss sticks are used during the Wealth God welcoming rituals performed during the night before the lunar new year; during such rituals very pungent and strong smells such as sandalwood are used.

Incense can also be used through the year. They are a powerful medium that can be used to clear the air of negatives; to suppress troublesome energies that bring aggravations that disturb the mind of residents.

Incense is usually associated with the transcendence of chi energy between cosmic realms of consciousness and are an advanced form of energy practices used in the old days by expert practitioners. They are powerful yet invisible instruments for dissolving concentrations of negative energy. The number 3 star is one example of a concentration of energy that brings aggravations. It is good feng shui to dissolve its effect.

An excellent way to stay immune to the 3 star therefore is to utilize calming aromas, and in the case of anyone staying in the North you can use incense for the outdoors and for your bedroom, you can try using lavender aroma which is relaxing and soothing when infused into the atmosphere.

What is more effective however is to perform the incense ritual which will get rid of anger vibrations very effectively. Incense also appease spiritual landlords in the area and they will help to suppress all negativities that cause hostile energy to burst into big quarrels. Burn sandalwood or pine incense regularly in the North in 2011.

Sandalwood incense is perfect for the North sector in 2011. Use sandalwood powder or specially packed concentrated sandalwood and use this to create smoke incense in a small charcoal burner. Once a week burn a little sandalwood incense in the North sector of the living area by literally lighting the fire. The result is a very calming influence in the home that brings harmony and happiness vibrations. This is a great modern way of dissolving the negative energies of the North in 2011.

Activating the Trinity of Tien Ti Ren

In the year 2011 **all four primary directional locations** - North, South, East and West - are afflicted, as we have seen with the illness, hostile, five yellow and natural disaster star. of the four only the West location has the lucky 9 star number but 9 in a Metal element sector always contains hidden dangers; so correcting, and placing remedies to safeguard the cardinal locations of the house is extremely important in 2011.

The **four secondary directions** on the other hand, are indicating extremely lucky star numbers, with 8 leading the way as it flies into the patriarchal corner of Northwest, followed by the heavenly 6 in the opposite direction of Southeast. Then there is the victory star in the Northeast and the star of romance and scholarship in the Southwest in 2011.

With this kind of star number configurations, we also note that the Northeast/Southwest axis (which is the favorable axis of this current period of 8) has been blessed with the star of earth seal in the SW and the matching counterpart star of the heaven seal in the Northeast.

The presence of these *heaven* and *earth* stars are indicative of the need for the trinity of lucky cosmic forces to be present in the North and the South, the other set of axis direction which are showing a set of two *Big Auspicious* stars. In N1 and N3 and also in S1 and S3, we see here a quartet of important lucky stars brought by the circle of the 24 mountains.

In 2011, there is the strong indication of substantial changes taking place in the world which will bring benefits to some and loss to others. This is vital to understand as the year itself is showing a set of four pillars which not only has 4 sets of clashing elements but also two yang and two yin pillars. This suggests that the complementarily of cosmic forces is balanced. Yin and yang are in balance.

Good fortune manifests as growth, sudden windfalls and big transformations of luck that bring a "*house filled with jewels*" enabling one to "*wear the jade belt*" if the household successfully activates the trinity of Tien Ti Ren. In other words, there must be plentiful supply of heaven, earth and mankind energies! This is something that is beneficial to ensure at all times but more so in 2011, where severe bad luck indications are balanced against equally powerful auspicious indications. So the important thing is to tap into the positive energies of the year, thereby getting on to the growth spiral. Tien ti ren is the key!

Symbolically, just placing the words heaven and earth are often good enough to complement the presence of people within a home. Mankind chi is the powerful yang chi that activates the yin earth chi and the cosmic heaven chi.

In the old days, wealthy households would always include miniature mountains to signify earth, and also all the deities of their faith - Taoism or Buddhism, the **8 Immortals** and the **18 holy beings** - all to signify heaven chi while at the same time imbuing their homes with activity and celebrations to signify mankind chi. This infusion of yang energy acts a catalyst to generate the presence of the powerful cosmic trinity.

In this way did wealthy households of the past live, and over the years, these practices came to signify the cultural underpinnings of the Chinese way of life. Thus one should not be surprised to note that many Chinese households believe that the blessing power of heaven is brought in by the presence of deities on their family altar. The family altar was always placed rather grandly, directly facing the front door.

This signified the continuing presence of heaven luck. It was important to keep the family altars clean with offerings of food, lights, water, wine and incense made daily. Wealthier households would even have professionals such as monks and holy men, who would come and recite prayers for the family at special dates in the year. These were daily rituals believed to keep the family patriarch safe and the household in a state of abundance. In other words, keeping their lifestyles secure.

In addition, good earth chi was assured by the presence of mountains and rivers simulated in landscaped gardens around the family home and symbolized by **mountain scenery paintings** inside the home. Good feng shui also ensures good chi flows in abundance through the rooms and corridors of the house.

Finally, excellent mankind chi is kept flowing fresh and revitalizing yang energy. Auspicious phrases and lucky rhyming couplets were placed as artistic calligraphy in important rooms of the house; this was the equivalent of today's very popular "*affirmations*".

The Chinese have been living with these powerful affirmations for as long as anyone can remember, and there are literally thousands of such lucky phrases such as "*your wealth has arrived*" or "*your luck is as long as the yellow river*"… and so forth.

The Chinese have been living with powerful affirmations
for as long as anyone can remember. These affirmations
often took the form of rhyming couplets, such as
"Your wealth is as long as the yellow river."

These are popular sayings exchanged between families during festive seasons and during Chinese New Year.

Anyone wanting to enjoy good fortune continuously must be mindful of the power generated by *tien ti ren* chi inside their homes. This is very timely for 2011 to help you benefit from the year. In 2011 therefore, the three dimensions of feng shui - space and time as well as the dimension which engages the cosmic force within the self (the purest source of yang energy generated from within you) must all be present. In fact, this is a major secret of feng shui. This is the mankind chi that pulls heaven and earth chi together.

Good mankind chi requires you to stay positive, to generate lucky aspirations and to anticipate good outcomes.

Your expectations must be high. You can enhance the empowerment of your own self. This unlocks for you the strength of mankind luck - *ren* chi - which pulls time and space into a powerful whole. With this kind of attitude, you can then start to enhance the four lucky secondary directions with powerful enhancing placement feng shui:

Enhancing the Chi of 8 in the Northwest

SE	SOUTH	SW
6	2	4
5	7	9
1	3	8 AUSPICIOUS
NE	NORTH	NW

The all-powerful and auspicious 8 flies to the place of the patriarch in 2011, bringing quite exceptional great good fortune to all the father figures of the world. Being located in the Northwest, the 8 Earth star also gets very considerably strengthened, and especially since it is flying to the Northwest from the center where it was located last year.

As an annual star number, the 8 is indeed very strong. It brings good relationship luck and it brings success and wealth. It is a powerful star at its zenith. What worked last year, the **crystal 8** embedded with real 24 carat gold, continues to work this year, so do display it in the Northwest of the house; or on your office.

But the crystal 8 becomes even more powerful when it is placed alongside a **crystal Ru Yi,** the scepter of authority. This is especially beneficial for Chief Executive Officers i.e. CEOs and bosses. In fact, anyone in a position of authority and power will benefit from the Ru Yi placed alongside the 8. In the old days, these symbols were recommended for mandarins at court - equivalent to the Ministers and top business leaders of today.

Those who want a boost to their career should definitely consider placing this powerful symbol of advancement and upward mobility in the Northwest corner of their home, of their office or their home office. With the 8 flying into the Northwest, the Ru Yi placed next to the 8 becomes especially effective. Place the **Ruyi** in exactly the middle of the Northwest sector i.e. in Northwest 2, as this is the auspicious part of this location.

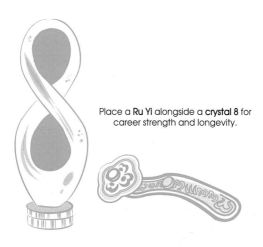

Place a **Ru Yi** alongside a **crystal 8** for career strength and longevity.

Activating the Power of Heavenly 6 in the Southeast

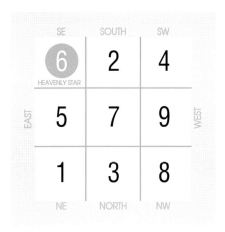

SE	SOUTH	SW
6 HEAVENLY STAR	2	4
5 (EAST)	7	9 (WEST)
1	3	8
NE	NORTH	NW

The number 6, a lucky white star usually associated with the cosmic energies of heaven, flies to the Southeast in 2011, directly facing the Northwest, thereby creating a powerful alliance between heaven and earth luck, bringing luck not only to the Southeast but also to the Northwest, directly opposite.

There is great synergy luck between father and eldest daughter in the family. Should either the master bedroom or the daughter's bedroom be located in the

Southeast, unexpected developments take place that lift the family fortunes higher than ever. The 6 star brings heaven's celestial blessings and good fortune for those blessed by its cosmic chi. This occurs when your bedroom is located in the Southeast; and if so, do make an effort to fill your room with yang chi energy, a higher noise level and perhaps greater movement in your room. In other words, make it vibrate with energy, as this will energize it, acting as a catalyst for good fortune to occur.

The number 6 signifies authority and power; it is associated with the management of economics and finances. At its peak, 6 stands for authority, influence and control over money, like being the Head of the Central Bank.

Appearing in the Southeast, it suggests financial management does well under a mature woman. Within the family, the year suggests that money should be handled by women and power by men. On balance, however, the male leader has greater strength than the female, but it is the woman who holds the purse strings. This is the way the energies are laid out for the year. Those observing this pattern of energy and flow with it are most likely to benefit from 2011.

It is beneficial to bring this auspicious 6 star to life as it really bring benefits to the entire household, especially in houses where the Southeast is not a tight corner or a small room that locks up its good energy.

To invoke the best kind of results from the 6 star in 2011 display the **Tree of Wealth** in the Southeast. Hang **six large coins** from the tree, and if there are also six birds on the tree, these signify exciting news coming to the household. The best way to create this symbolic effect is to find a healthy growing tree and to place it in the Southeast before hanging all the auspicious symbols that ignite the intrinsic power of 6. Remember, 6 birds and six large coins will attract heaven luck.

Display the **Tree of Wealth** in the Southeast in 2011.

Enhancing Victory Luck in the NE

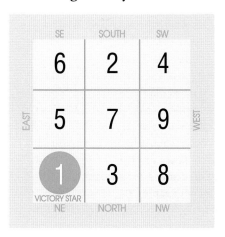

The number 1 star which brings triumph and success flies to the Northeast corner in 2011 and for those whose bedroom or main door is located here, it is beneficial for the symbolic **banner of victory** to be placed here. This also benefits anyone residing in this part of the house for whom this lucky star number brings victory. The number 1 star attracts all kinds of triumphant moments. This kind of luck is especially welcome by those engaged in competitive pursuits as it helps you win.

In 2011, the Victory Star brings winning luck to young men, especially those who are ambitious and keen to succeed.

What is exciting is that the direction Northeast benefits from three good stars of the 24 mountains, so there is some very exciting potential that can be tapped from this location. It is a good idea to keep the Northeast energized through the year. Do not let it get too quiet. Yang energy should be created by making sure this part of the house or of your favorite room stays well lit and is occupied. At all costs, prevent *yin spirit formation* by not keeping the sector too silent through the year.

The most auspicious symbols to place here in the Northeast are all the symbols that signify victory such as awards, certificates, trophies and victory banners. You can also fly a flag in the Northeast sector this year. The flag always suggests the announcement of victories.

Enhance the Victory Star of 1 in the Northeast this year with a **Banner of Victory**.

Benefitting from the Star of Scholarship and Romance in the Southwest

The fourth lucky secondary location of 2011 is the Southwest, which benefits from the romance and scholastic star of 4. This very powerful star will bring beautiful romantic energy to anyone residing in the Southwest

This is, in any case, the location associated with marriage and domestic happiness. It is also the place of the mother, so the matriarchal force is associated with the Southwest. With the romantic star 4 here, all the stress and strains associated with the *five yellow* of the past year has definitely dissolved.

SE	SOUTH	SW
6	2	4
5	7	9
1	3	8
NE	NORTH	NW

EAST — WEST

In 2011, the Southwest brings enhanced love and marriage opportunities. It also brings better harmony and appreciation of the mother figure within families and households.

The number 4 is often associated with romantic peach blossom vibrations, so the luck of this sector directly benefits those still single and unmarried. For those already married, peach blossom brings a happier family life. Domestic energies get enhanced and those who know how to energize the Southwest with bright lights will find the number 4 star jazzing up their love relationships.

Scholastic Luck

Those residing in the Northeast part of the house also benefit from the other influences brought by the number 4 star. These benefits are related to scholastic and literary pursuits, and the star brings good academic luck to those having their bedroom here. Facing Northeast is also beneficial for students and those sitting for examinations. The Northeast stands for wisdom and learning, so this is a very positive star here. The only problem will be that love can also be a distraction, so if you want to enhance the scholastic side of this star, you should place literary symbols here.

Anyone involved in a writing or literary career will also benefit from being located in the Northeast. But do make sure you activate the sector with bright lights. Fire element energy is excellent to add to the strength of the sectors' good luck. Doing so strengthens both the romance as well as the scholastic dimensions of your fortunes in 2011. So light up this corner as best you can!

The **Chi Lin with 4 scholastic impliments** is a fabulous energizer of Education Luck.

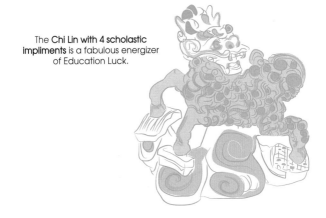

Magnifying the Earth Element to Enhance Resources

Updating feng shui each year involves more than taking care of lucky and unlucky sectors. It also requires being alert to the balance of elements and their effects on the year's energy flows. This is revealed in the year's four pillars chart which in 2011 indicates an absence of the Earth element in the primary chart of the year.

The intrinsic element of the year as indicated by the heavenly stem of the DAY pillar is yang Metal, and altogether there are 3 Metal elements in the chart. There are also three Wood elements, one Water and one Fire, making then a total of the eight elements that make up the primary chart of the year.

Earth element is thus missing in 2011 and the Earth element symbolizes resources. This makes Earth a very important element, because without resources, none of the other indicated attributes such as wealth, success, prosperity, creativity and so forth can manifest.

This is one of the secrets in Paht Chee reading. It is always important that the intrinsic element (in this year, it is Metal) is kept continually replenished by having the element that produces it present. In 2011, this means the Earth element, because Earth produces Metal; hence Earth is the resource element for 2011 - do note that this changes from year to year.

As Earth is the missing element this year, it is important that anyone who makes the effort to magnify the presence of Earth element in their living spaces is bound to enjoy excellent feng shui. And Earth element is best symbolized by either a **picture of mountains** or better yet, having the presence of crystals, stones and rocks which come from within the earth.

Create a mountain of pebbles in your home to activate the all-important resource element of Earth in 2011. The NE and SW activated this way brings valuable hidden resource luck to the home.

This is the key that unlocks the manifestation of other kinds of luck for you. It is important to create the presence of Earth element objects in the home and to also strengthen the Earth element corners of the home. These are the Southwest and the Northeast. Keep these corners of the home well lit so that the Fire element is forever present to make these Earth element sectors strong.

The paht chee chart does however show that there is hidden Earth but here the Earth element is not immediately available. Nevertheless, it does indicate the availability of hidden resources. When the Earth element gets magnified the economics of your living situation becomes extremely comfortable.

So do place stones, rocks or crystals - the best are the large circular crystal globes - on your coffee table in the living area and then shine a light on it so that the energy of the Earth element gets diffused through the room. Also enhance all compass Earth sectors - Notheast and Southwest as well as the center - in the same way. Creating a "*mountain*" with rocks or pebbles in an artistic way also brings excellent feng shui potential.

Indeed, it is not only the Chinese who have tradition of creating "*miniature mountains*" in and around their gardens and homes. Many other Eastern traditions where feng shui is popularly practiced - such as Japan and Korea - also have their own artistic recreations of mountain scenery. This always signifies the Earth element.

Hidden Earth

We need to also look at the entire paht chee chart to highlight the element that is in most short supply; this involves looking at all the elements of the year's chart including the hidden elements. In 2011, there are three elements of hidden Earth which then brings about a magnification of the Earth element. But in expanding the analysis to include the hidden elements, we need to also take note of the shortage of the Water element. So as in the previous year, the Water element continues to be needed. But in this respect, 2011 is better than 2010, because this year there is one Water element available (last year Water was completely missing). The Hour pillar has yang Water as its heavenly stem.

But Water needs to be supplemented to keep the elements in good balance.

Adding to the strength of Water would strengthen to the Wood element for the year and this would be beneficial. This is because Wood symbolizes prosperity and financial success. Hence the placement or addition of the Water element in the Wood sectors East and Southeast would create excellent **wealth feng shui**.

Under the Eight Aspirations formula of feng shui, the Southeast is also the sector that stands for prosperity via the accumulation of wealth. To activate this sector, water is required, but water without earth is not as effective as water *with* earth!

So what is required is the placement of a **crystal water feature** in the Southeast corner. This would be an excellent wealth energizer for 2011. Any kind of water presence for this corner in any room that you frequently use (except your bedroom) would be excellent feng shui. Next place a **small image** of **your own animal sign** near the water. This will help you through the year as the presence of water near your sign is symbolically very fruitful.. For the Rabbit born, this brings a double benefit because the Rabbit's earthly branch is the Wood element, which gets stronger with water.

Nine Wealth Gods
to Materialize Prosperity Luck

The final feng shui tip we would like to share with readers for the year is the placement of a ship bringing nine wealth gods sailing into your home. This has great relevance for the year as it suggests that the winds and waters will bring the divine personifications of wealth luck into the home.

Wealth Gods are a very effective for symbolic placement in feng shui folklore, and it is for this reason that the Chinese always invite Wealth Deities into the home.

But there are certain years when the Wealth gods are especially effective and that is when the *Big Auspicious* stars of the 24 mountains fly into two opposite primary directions, which is the case in 2011.

Both the North and the South sectors of every home have, and thus can benefit from these stars; but they work only if they can be energized by the presence of Wealth Deities which are believed to bring good cosmic chi into the homes. This will activate the North-South axis. So do place the ship in a North-South orientation within the home.

Powerful Talismans & Amulets For 2011

Part 7

If you have been following the advice given in these Fortune & Feng Shui books on annual feng shui updates, you are already familiar with the time dimension of feng shui which protects against negative luck each year.

This requires overall cleansing and re-energizing of the energy of the home to prepare for the coming of a new year, while simultaneously making placement changes to accommodate a new pattern of chi distribution. Getting rid of old items and replacing with specially made new remedial cures that are in tune with the year's chi brings pristine and fresh new luck into the home.

This year the Rabbit person needs to be more careful. You are surrounded by the Five Yellow star and also face the Three Killings affliction coming from opposite you from the West. You also have the Tai Sui of the year in your location of East, so it is important that you have him on your side. This is a year to tread carefully. Stay well protected and think defensive first before looking to activate for good luck. Don't be in a hurry for wealth or success or you could get burnt in the process. On the other hand, there is no reason you cannot achieve some personal victories and triumphs if you navigate the year carefully and utilize the necessary protective talismans.

Dispel Three Killings Chi with the 3 Celestial Protectors

The three celestial guardians are the best cure for the Three Killings affliction, which directly faces your home direction of East in 2011. Depicted with their implements, the Chi Lin carries the Lasso, the Fu Dog carries the Hook, while the Pi Yao has the Sword. Together these three guardians will dispel the negative energy coming your way from this affliction, protecting against loss of relationships, loss of good name and loss of wealth. Display them in the West part of your living room or home and also in the West of your office.

Transform the Five Yellow into a Wealth-Bringing Star

The Rabbit is overwhelmed by the Five Yellow affliction this year, which occupies both your home location of East as well as featuring in your 24 mountains constellation. This is the main affliction you need to worry about this year, so it is vitally important to work at keeping it under control. The best cure for this is the Five Element Pagoda with the Tree of Life.

This Pagoda features the tree of life growing from the base right to the top of the pagoda, with three pairs of birds sitting on its branches. The jewels hanging off its branches signify the Earth element, which brings wealth in 2011. Because you are short of lucky stars in your chart this year, you need to look at ways to tap indirect wealth. This cure transforms your bad luck into good luck, turning the afflictive energies in your chart into positive energies. This powerful 5 element pagoda then becomes a transforming tool which turns the all-powerful *wu wang* into a wealth-bringing star for you.

Strengthen Personal Energy with the Crystal Water Talisman

Water is the element that is terribly lacking in the 2011 Paht Chee chart, and carrying a symbol of Water is what will attract success into your life. The Rabbit especially will benefit from this talisman, as your intrinsic element is Wood, and Water produces Wood. Having this element with you at all times will thus not only add potency to your success luck, allowing good opportunities to translate into results for you, but it will also fuel your self element of Wood, thus strengthening you personally.

Attract Mentor Support with the Heaven Seal Activator

The Rabbit is in need of any help it can get this year. When you're short on good stars in your chart, you need to make the very most of any opportunities that come your way, and the help of influential people who can help you can make all the difference. Carry the Heaven Luck Activator to ensure you can spot good opportunities when they come along, and to help you make the most of these opportunities. This talisman has been designed with the image of the Jade Heaven

Emperor on one side and the Chien Trigram on the other, bringing you prosperity luck *"as vast as the skies."*

Make Best Use of Positive Affirmations to Unleash the Power of your Subconscious

Positive words and affirmations when viewed over and over are like mantras that enter your subconscious. This year we have incorporated these affirmative and positive sayings into several of our new items as powerful activators of good luck. Our glass pebbles and mandala stones with positive words and auspicious symbols can be displayed in your animal sign location of East for best effect. Choose stones with words or pictures that hold special meaning for you. Put them in a pot or bowl in the East, or even better, load them onto a miniature sailing ship, letting the ship sail in from one of your good directions. You can also add these stones into your mandala offering set, if you have one.

Sacred Moving Mantra Watches

Moving mantra watches are suitable for any animal sign; anyone can wear them. These watches have been specially designed to bring you the trinity of luck - heaven, earth and mankind luck. There are 3 clocks in this watch, so it can support 3 time zones, but even better, around each dial is a mantra which moves, so every second that passes is like chanting an auspicious mantra. The mantras featured on this watch are the Amitabha Buddha mantra, Manjushri mantra and the Kuan Yin mantra. Wearing this watch will bring protection as well as attract plenty of good fortune and prosperity continuously into your life.

Also available this year are the **Medicine Buddha watch** and the **Green Tara** watch.

The **Medicine Buddha watch** has been specially designed to bring good health and longevity, and it comes with the Medicine Buddha mantra and image. The band is embossed with the Medicine Buddha mantra. The mantra is repeated on the face in a moving dial so the mantra is constantly moving. Wearing this watch will bring you protection from sickness. Suitable for those of you who may be prone to falling sick, or the more elderly among you, to maintain a long, healthy and comfortable life.

The **Green Tara watch** features the beautiful Green Tara in the face. The band of the watch is stamped with Green Tara's mantra - Om Tare Tuttare Ture Soha. This mantra is repeated in a dial on the face which is constantly moving, creating blessings for you all hours of the night and day. Green Tara brings success luck and helps to overcome blocks and obstacles to success. She is also known as the Swift Liberator, known to bring results quickly to those who call on her help.

Table Top Treasures to Enhance Desks and Workspaces

Many of us spend a great deal of our time at our desks and in front of our computers whether during work, play or our spare time. It is always good to energize the immediate space around us with good fortune symbols and items that hold positive meaning for us. We have designed two such items that make simply the most delightful table top treasures, a **miniature photo frame** enameled with peonies, the flower of love, and a **matching clock**. Place photos of your loved ones in such photo frames near you while you work. This will bring you positive and happy energy, and when you're happy, you become more productive, more peaceful and yes, also more lucky.

Powerful Gemstones
to Connect Your Lucky Day
with the Seven Most Powerful Planets

The seven planets signify seven days of the week, and connection with each planet is achieved by wearing its correct gemstone. Using your lucky day of the week, you can determine which planet has the luckiest influence on you and which gemstone you should wear or carry close to your body to attract the good luck of that planet. Start wearing the gem on your lucky day and empower with incense and mantras before wearing.

The SUN is the planet of Sunday

This is the principal planet which gives light and warmth, brings fame and recognition and enhances one's personal aura. It is an empowering planet that brings nobility, dignity and power. This gemstone enhances your leadership qualities and increases your levels of confidence so your mind is untroubled and clear. The color that activates the SUN is RED, so all red-colored gemstones are excellent for those of you having SUNDAY as your lucky day based on your Lunar Mansion.

Rubies, red garnets, rubellites or even **red glass** or **crystal** would be extremely powerful. You can also wear red clothes, carry red handbags to enhance the energy of the Sun, but a red gemstone is the most powerful... Start wearing on a Sunday at sunrise after reciting the mantra here 7 times.

Mantra: *Om Grini Suraya Namah Hum Phat*

The MOON is the planet of Monday

The moon has a powerful influence on your mind, your thoughts and attitudes. Lunar energy is associated with the tides and with water, bringing enormous good fortune to those who successfully activate its positive influences; and is especially suitable for those whose lucky day is Monday.

For energizing lunar energy, the best is to wear the pearl, those created in the deep seas or from the freshwater of rivers. Wearing pearls (any color) bring good habits to the wearer and creates good thoughts. It brings calm, peace of mind, mental stability and good health. It also brings wealth and enhances all positive thoughts. Over time, it engenders the respect of others. Start wearing on a Monday in the evening before sunset and recite the mantra here 11 times.

Mantra: *Om Som Somaya Namah Hum Phat*

The Planet MARS rules Tuesday

This is a masculine planet associated with fiery energy and the power of oratory. Activating Mars brings an authoritative air of leadership and confidence like a general leading troops to war. It brings success and victory in any competitive situation. Worn on a Tuesday, a gemstone that resonates with Mars unleashes all its fiery strength in competitive situations. The most powerful gemstone to activate Mars is **natural red coral,** the deeper the red, the better it will be. Start wearing on a Tuesday one hour after sunrise and after reciting the mantra here 19 times.

Mantra: *Om Ang Anghara Kaya Namah Hum Phat*

The Planet MERCURY rules Wednesdays

To anyone who can successfully activate Mercury, this planet brings great intelligence and amazing analytical capabilities that become vastly enhanced. Mercury increases your ability to learn and your powers of absorption are magnified. The ability to memorize also improves. Mercury facilitates powers of expression and communication. You will work fast and become effective in getting things done. The cosmic color of Mercury is green; **emeralds, green tourmalines, green quartz** are all suitable. **Green jade** is the most powerful

energizer of Mercury. Anyone wearing jade will always
be smarter than others and can always outwit anyone.
It is a very powerful gemstone. Start wearing on a
Wednesday two hours after sunrise and recite the
mantra here 9 times.

Mantra: *Om Bhrum Buddhaya Namah Hum Phat*

The Planet Jupiter rules Thursdays

The most auspicious of the seven planets, this planet
attracts wealth and brings great influence to those
who can successfully activate its powerful energies.
To do so requires you to perform many charitable
works and then you will need to wear the gemstone of
Jupiter that will make you rise to spectacular heights
of success. You will become a highly respected leader
wielding power and great influence.

Jupiter's energies are transmitted through yellow
gemstones the most powerful of which are **yellow
sapphires, citrines, topaz** or **flawless yellow-coloured
glass** or **crystal.** Wear a yellow sapphire that is flawless
and is at least 7 carats big. This brings enormous
wealth luck. **Yellow Citrines** or **Imperial Topaz** are
also effective. But they must be flawless or you will
be quick-tempered and hard to please. Start wearing

on a Thursday an hour before sunset after reciting the mantra here 19 times.

Mantra: *Om Bhrim Bhrihas Pataye Namah Hum Phat*

The Planet Venus rules Fridays

This is the planet of love, romance, sexuality, marriage, material comforts, domestic bliss and luxury. Venus brings all kinds of artistic skills to those whose lucky day is Friday and also to those who empower Venus by connecting to it via the wearing of its gemstones. Venus transmits its cosmic energy through **flawless diamonds, quartz crystals, zircons, white sapphires,** and other **colorless gemstones** with **clear transparency**.

Various subtle hues such as pink, yellow and blue tints are suitable for different types of professions and social positions, as long as the gem does not have any solid color. So it is crystalline stones that resonate best with Venus. Start wearing on a Friday at sunrise after you recite the mantra here 16 times.

Mantra: *Om Shum Shukraya Namah Hum Phat*

The Planet Saturn rules Saturdays

This planet governs careers and an empowered or energized Saturn is excellent for overcoming obstacles at the work place. When projects or bosses cause you to stumble or when hindrances stand in the way, it is because Saturn has to be appeased. Those whose lucky day is Friday possess the ability to rise above hardships and obstacles, but enhancing Saturn by wearing its gemstone will empower you even more. Anyone wearing **Blue Sapphires** can connect directly with Saturn.

Start wearing on a Saturday 2 and a half hours before sunset and recite the mantra here 23 times.

Mantra: *Om Sham Shanay Scaraya Namah Hum Phat*

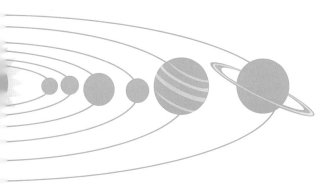

So, What Do You Think?

We hope you enjoyed this book and gained some
meaningful insights about your own personal
horoscope and animal sign... and you've put some
of our feng shui recommendations into practice!
Hopefully you are already feeling a difference
and enjoying the results of the positive actions
you have taken.

But Don't Stop Now!

You can receive the latest weekly news and
feng shui updates from Lillian herself absolutely
FREE! Learn even more of her secrets and
open your mind to the deeper possibilities of
feng shui today.

Lillian too's free online weekly ezine is
now AVAILABLE

Here's how easy it is to subscribe:
Just go online to www.lilliantoomandalaezine.com
and sign up today!

Your newsletter will be delivered automatically
to your website.

And there's more!

When you subscribe to my FREE Mandala
Weekly Ezine you will receive a special
personalized BONUS report from me... but it's
only available for those who register online at
www.lilliantoomandalaezine.com!

DON'T BE LEFT OUT! Join Today!

Thank you for investing in yourself and in this
book. Join me online every week and learn how
easy it is to make good feng shui a way of life!